The Young Man of Character

The Young Man of Character

BISHOP TIHAMER TOTH

Translated by Gyula Mago

Angelus
Press

2915 Forest Avenue | Kansas City, MO 64109

Library of Congress Cataloging-in-Publication Data

Tóth, Tihamér, 1889-1939.
  [Jellemes ifjú. English]
  The young man of character / Tihamér Tóth ; translated by Gyula Mago.
     p. cm.
  ISBN 978-1-937843-02-1
  1. Character--Religious aspects--Christianity. 2. Young men--Conduct of
life. I. Title.
  BV4599.5.C45T6813 2012
  248.8'32--dc23

                                    2012007081

ANGELUS PRESS

2915 FOREST AVENUE
KANSAS CITY, MISSOURI 64109
PHONE (816) 753-3150
FAX (816) 753-3557
ORDER LINE 1-800-966-7337
www.angeluspress.org

ISBN: 978-1-937843-02-1
FIRST PRINTING–June 2012
SECOND PRINTING–April 2016

Printed in the United States of America

Contents

Preface

Man, as created by God, has his feet in two worlds at once, the natural world and the supernatural world. Adam was created in grace; he was never meant to live for even a moment in a purely natural world. His life on this earth was meant, as is ours after him, to be not only a test, but also and essentially a preparation for the life of union with God in heaven. Thus God infused a participation in His own life into Adam's soul, and Adam's mission on earth was to protect and develop that life of grace. He failed, losing grace not only for himself, but also for us, and that loss left his nature deeply wounded, and ours after him.

The mission of Our Lord Jesus Christ consisted in restoring souls to the life of grace: "I am come that they may have life, and have it more abundantly." To that end He died, and to that end He left us the sacraments, source of supernatural life. We received the life of grace on the day of our baptism, and our mission on earth is to protect and develop that life of grace. Such is our goal, and no other human objective has any worth but insofar as it helps us attain that goal.

Grace, however, is incarnated, so to speak, in nature–nature is the foundation upon which the supernatural edifice of the soul is built. And that foundation, as we have said, was wounded–deeply–by the fall of Adam. The Christian man has always been obliged to take into account the weakness of his fallen nature. No man who wishes to be strong in grace can afford to neglect the foundation upon which grace builds: he must work incessantly to stabilize that foundation by the acquisition of virtue–discipline of mind, heart, and will. This work has never been more necessary than today, however, for the enemy of souls, having from long date succeeded in ridding the world almost completely of the life of grace, has now succeeded in creating an unnatural world that attacks directly the nature the man.

The great Cardinal Pie, writing nearly 150 years ago, lamented the scarcity of true men already in the world of his time: "Is not ours an age of mislived lives, of unmanned men?" he wrote. "The world is dwindling away for lack of men; the nations are perishing for scarcity of men, for the rareness of men."

Bishop Toth, writing many years after, echoed Cardinal Pie's lament, and by the volume in your hands sought to help remedy the problem. His focus is primarily on fortifying and rebuilding the natural foundation, preferring, as he explains at the end of his book, to save for another volume his treatment of the supernatural life. It was, one might justly maintain, an unfortunate decision, for although we must distinguish natural from supernatural virtue, we cannot, in the real order of things, separate them. Just as man was never intended by God to live on a merely natural level, so virtue to be complete must be both natural and supernatural–we must work always on both levels. On a natural level, a man must strive, by the persevering repetition of virtuous actions, to acquire virtuous habits. His efforts even on a natural level, however, must be determined by a supernatural desire to conform himself in all things to Our Lord Jesus Christ–this is his true end, the purpose for which he was created. And that end, being a supernatural one, is impossible to attain without constant recourse to Christ by prayer and by reception of the sacraments.

Thus Cardinal Pie, lamenting, as we said, the scarcity of true men, emphasized that the solution is to be found only in a return to God. "There are no men," he wrote, "where there is no character; there is no character where there are no principles, doctrines, stands taken; there are no stands taken, no doctrines, no principles, where there is no religious faith and consequently no religion in society. Do what you will: only from God will you get men." And Bishop Toth would agree: "A truly strong character must be founded on Christ, and the whole life must be built on Him."

The present volume, while it does not emphasize this crucial reality, is nevertheless of precious worth. Appealing with conviction and enthusiasm to the noble aspirations placed in the heart of every young man by God, Bishop Toth's writings are highly motivating, and his message begs a response from the first page:

Every man cannot be expected to be rich; neither can everybody be expected to be learned or famous; but everybody can be expected to have a good character. Few men are born to be conquerors. Few men are born to be leaders of countries. But to conquer the realm of the soul, and to gain the crown of manly character, this lofty task awaits each one of us. Each and every one. (p. 1)

You have a treasure in you more valuable than anything conceivable: your immortal soul. The task of your earthly life is to make your soul the most ideal, the most beautiful, the richest in noble qualities. Your eternal life will correspond to the perfection of your soul that you managed to accomplish in this earthly life. (p. 173)

With clarity and a noble vision grounded by common sense, Bishop Toth examines point by point the various characteristics of a manly character. He has a gift for vividly illustrating each point, this one by an anecdotal jewel, that one by an inspiring quote. In the end, he succeeds remarkably not only in making clear the path to be followed, but also in stirring the will to desire it.

Thus we have here a volume very much worth putting into the hands of our young men. May it prove to be of value in the critical work of rebuilding Christendom, one soul at a time.

Fr. Gerard Beck, SSPX

The man who is just and firm to his purpose

If the broken world should fall to pieces,

The ruins would strike him undismayed.

Regulus in Carthage

Carthage sent a delegation to Rome suing for peace. The delegation was led by the Roman prisoner Regulus, from whom they extracted an oath that he would return to his captivity if unsuccessful in his negotiations. Imagine his struggles during the mission to his beloved Rome! He could have stayed home in Rome if peace were established.

But do you know what he did? He most strongly urged the continuation of fighting, and when the Roman Senate encouraged him to stay home saying that his oath was extracted by force and therefore not binding, he answered: "You insist that I lose my honor? I know that if I return, torture and death await me. But what are they compared to the shame of dishonor, compared to the wounds of a sinful soul? Although a prisoner of Carthage, I want to preserve my Roman honor intact. I swore that I would return. I will do so. Let us leave the rest to the gods."

He returned, and indeed he was executed after severe tortures. He was a Roman of character! But then how much more ought to be expected of a Christian of character!

Every man cannot be expected to be rich; neither can everybody be expected to be learned or famous; but everybody can be expected to have a good character. Few men are born to be conquerors. Few men are born to be leaders of countries. But to conquer the realm of the soul and to gain the crown of manly character, this lofty task awaits everybody. Everybody. Many do not do it. But I hope you will do it, my son!

But character is not like the top prize in lottery–to be gained without deserving it. Character is not like an aristocratic name–to be inherited without effort. Character is the result of hard struggle, of self-education, of self-denial, of manly spiritual combat. This is a struggle everybody has to fight until victory is gained.

Character is the result of this struggle. What this means may be hard to grasp at this stage. But once you stand before God and the veil is finally removed from the chief accomplishment of your life, and you see the magnificence of your own soul on which you worked so much you will cry like Haydn at the performance of his oratorio *The Creation*: "My God, have I really done this?"

Homines sunt voluntates, says St. Augustine with remarkable brevity: men are their wills. The worth of man is given by his will. It is increasingly realized that schools today, by merely imparting knowledge, put an exaggerated emphasis on the intellect and neglect the development of character and will power. The sad result is that society has more educated brains than firm backbones, more knowledge than character. Yet, the mainstay and foundation of the state is not science, but morality; not wealth, but honor; not cowardliness, but character.

This book aims to train young men of character whose thinking is "I have an awesome responsibility for the task before me, the moral development of my soul. By fulfilling my duties throughout an exemplary life, I have to develop my soul into a beautiful flower that can stand worthily before God for all eternity."

This book aims to train young men of character during these times when the whole world seems to be upside down. These days, when the chief illness of mankind is the frightening atrophy of will power (the source of all sins); when lack of character is called clever adaptability; when denial of principles is called realpolitik; when pursuing selfish interests is called the common good; when the hypersensitive taking offense over everything is called self-respect; when envy is called love of justice; when hard work is avoided under the pretext of being impossible; when everybody is pursuing comfort, enjoyment and pleasure–this book aims to train young men of character, with firm principles and with will power not deterred by obstacles; young men who are knights dedicated to their duty; young men with souls that are firm like steel, straight like the truth, bright like the sunlight, and clear like a mountain stream.

This book aims to train young men of character during these times teeming with distorted souls, when the vast majority of students have no interest in spiritual problems; whose only concern is how to outwit their teachers, how to play hooky, who the latest celebrities are, and how to find the best parties. So many of these! And so few young men of character! Yet this book will want to demonstrate that nevertheless those few are in the right.

The many look so merry and carefree, whereas the few are working hard to blaze the trail of character; yet this book urges you to join the latter, because that is the only way worthy of a human being. I hold with Schiller (1759-1805): "Men are made great or insignificant by their wills" (*The Death of Wallenstein*). And I also hold with Baron József Eötvös (1813-1871), the great Hungarian thinker: "The worth of a man depends not on the strength of his intellect, but on the strength of his will. Great intellectual abilities will only weaken the one who lacks strength of will; and there is no more unfortunate creature than a great intellect without the corresponding character."

The farmer inspects his land at springtime, slowly reflecting: "My land! what are you going to give me this year?" The land answers in return: "First you tell me what you are going to give me!"

Similarly, the youth before the gate of his own life asks: "Life! what are you going to give me? What am I to expect?" And his life answers in return: "It depends on what you are going to give me! As you work, so shall you receive. As you sow, so shall you reap."

This book will teach you the means of self-education. This book will point out the dangers, it will give you the tools, but does not do the fighting for you. If you want to become a young man of character, you have to perform all the required spiritual labor yourself. You will find that the road to building character is not an easy road. It takes a strong will to be permanently at war with your errors, light and grave, with no cessation of the hostilities ever to be allowed.

> You have to be determined, you have to will strongly!
> You have to rule your senses and emotions.
> You have to put order into your thoughts.
> You have to first think, then speak.
> You have to first reflect, then act.
> You have to learn from the past, consider the future, and use the present well.
> You have to work willingly, endure patiently, live an upright life, and some day die in peace expecting eternal happiness.

Is there a loftier program for your life? Is there a worthier goal to live for? May this book help many young men in the exalted task of shaping their characters.

CHAPTER ONE

Who Is the Young Man of Character?

What is character? What do we mean when we say: this is a young man of character? By character we mean the steadfastness of the human will directed towards the good; a young man of character has noble principles and will not compromise them even if sticking to them involves sacrifices.

By contrast, a wavering, unreliable young man of weak character or of no character is the one who changes his principles to correspond to circumstances, to friends, to acquaintances, one who abandons his ideals as soon as he encounters resistance.

This reveals the nature of character development. First you have to acquire noble ideals and principles, then you have to train yourself by constant practice always to act according to them in all circumstances. Whoever does not have principles is like a reed in a storm. Today he does this, tomorrow he does that. So the first task is to embrace firm principles, then to develop the strength to follow them.

The first task then is to develop the right principles. What is the right principle for studying? "I have to study diligently, with perseverance, because God expects me to develop the talents given to me."

What is the right principle towards my fellow men? "As you would have men treat you, you are to treat them." And so on. You should have a correct principle in everything.

The second, and harder, task is always to follow these right principles, that is, to develop your character. Character is not given as a gift; one has to earn it with decades of thorough, painstaking work. Your character may be influenced by your environment, inherited traits, good or bad qualities, but ultimately it is your personal creation, the result of your self-education. Everybody receives two kinds of education: one from parents and schools, and the other, the more important one, from ourselves.

Do you know what formation is? It is influencing the human will so that it will pursue the good in every situation with certainty and gladness.

Do you know what character is? It is a consistent way of acting that follows firm principles, the steadiness of the will in the service of ideals recognized as true, the persevering steadfastness of a soul in the service of a noble conception of life.

So, as you can see, the hard part is not embracing the right principles, rather it is following them unwaveringly. "This is my principle, and I shall remain loyal to it no matter what it costs!" And since remaining loyal is usually costly, that is why there are so few men of character.

"Remain always loyal to your principles," "always stick with the truth," and so on. Who would not get enthusiastic about such thoughts? If only it were easier to realize these thoughts. The resistance of society, friends, fashions, and my own selfish self easily make all these plans go up in smoke.

Read how the poet Robert Reinick (1805-1852) warns you:

> Be not a weather vane
> And do not always start new things.
> What you have set out to do
> In that persist until the end.

This is where the correct self-education will help you.

Form Yourself!

To create in your soul the sublime picture God envisioned of you–this is the lofty work of self-formation. You have to do this yourself, nobody can do this for you. Others can give you advice, point out the right road, but eventually you have to feel the desire to realize the sublime picture God has hidden in your soul. You have to have the desire to become noble, strong, and pure. You have to know what your soul is like, what is weak in it, what is missing from it.

You have to prepare for the work of forming your soul, and you will have to understand that success will be achieved only through effort, self-denial, and self-conquest. Often you will have to deny yourself pleasant things, often you will have to do things not to your liking, persevere with clenched lips, defying everything even when a good intention leads to failure over and over again.

Your character, the outcome of your whole life depends on such small things.

> Sow a thought, and you shall reap a desire;
> sow a desire, and you shall reap an act;
> sow an act, and you shall reap a habit;
> sow a habit, and you shall reap a character;
> sow a character, and you shall reap your fate.

Indeed, small thoughts and acts may determine your destiny.

The Hungarian poet Ferenc Kölcsey (1790-1838) wrote: "In every hour of your life turn your sight with respect and admiration towards virtue; never pass up an opportunity to do good, even though this act would go against your desires and would not be to your advantage; train your will to conquer the resistance: this is how you will build character to accomplish great things for your age and for the future so that you may be honored by your fellow men."

But the human will has to be adjusted to the Divine Will also. There is no more sublime training of the will than to be able to say with conviction: yet not my will, but thine be done (Luke 22:42). There is no more valuable self-formation than to ask, following our deeds, words, and thoughts: "Lord, was my act or word indeed according to Your holy will?"

So start forming your character now, while you are young. If you grow up, it will be too late. Character cannot be developed in the confusion of life. If one enters the whirling of the world without a firm character, he will even lose the little he had upon entering.

Ein Herz von Erz

By now you know who is called a young man of character: the one who has noble ideals and principles, and who is able to remain faithful to them. Even if he is the only one in the whole world to hold them. Even if everybody around him lacks character. To remain faithful despite contrary bad examples. To remain faithful under all circumstances: this can be very trying.

When cruel boys, like bloodhounds, mercilessly irritate a weaker companion, and he, like a defenseless deer before hound dogs, is looking for help in vain, then gently divert the conversation and disarm the cruel intentions. This is bravery, consistency of principle, and love. *Ein Herz von Erz!*

When immature teenagers pour ridicule and scorn on the holiest truths of our religion, and using "arguments" found in cheap, obscure books amid crude laughter try to refute the teachings of the catechism class, then to stand up to it bravely, and without giving personal offense, by exposing the sophistry and confusion with superior knowledge, to speak in defense of the religious truth just ridiculed–that requires heroism and character.

When you hear the carefree laughter of your schoolmates under your window calling you to join them away from the forbidding algebra problem you are struggling with, then to remain faithful to your duties–that requires character. *Ein Herz von Erz!*

During the persecutions of the first Christian centuries a simple farmer was captured and placed in front of the statue of Jupiter. "Throw some incense into the fire and thereby adore our gods!" "No, I will not do that," replied quietly Barlaam (Roman Martyrology, November 19). He resisted torturing. They put incense into his hand and forcibly stretched his arm so that his hand was over the flame. "Drop the incense into the flame and you are free!" "No, I will not do that," replied Barlaam. The flames burned through his hand, the incense burned in his burning hand, yet martyr Barlaam did not deny his God. *Ein Herz von Erz!*

How few of us have the characters of potential martyrs! The characters admired even by Horace when he wrote:

> The man who is just and firm to his purpose
> If the broken world should fall to pieces,
> The ruins would strike him undismayed.

The soldier in Pompeii who was on duty guarding a gate at the outbreak of Vesuvius: everything was engulfed in volcanic matter, everything was being destroyed, but he the soldier did not move, was found there spear in hand, faithful unto death.

You see this firm backbone, this consistency of principle, this raised forehead–this is what we call character.

When I look around I see very different types. I see students covered with perfume walking down the promenade. I see the ones who live in movie theaters. I see the ones who live at parties. I see the ones smoking cigarettes. I see the ones whose only reading is the sports paper. I see the idlers and the slackers. And the innumerable students who are supposed to learn, yet learning nothing.

The Words of Epictetus

Even the honest, thinking pagan realized that although one may be a famous scientist, a great artist, a world famous sportsman or an extremely wealthy man, without character he is worth nothing.

Read what Epictetus (A.D. 55-135), a Greek Stoic philosopher born as a slave wrote:

Think of satisfying your soul
  rather than your stomach.
    (*Gnomologium Epicteteum* 20. ed. Schenkl–Teubner. Leipzig, 1898-1899)

Die rather than live a morally unsatisfactory life.
  (Fragm. 32, 422)

Whether your body is bound
  depends on the accidents of your fate;
if your soul is bound you have a moral flaw.
You are a slave if your body is free but your soul is bound;
  you are free if your body is bound but your soul
is not bound by depravity.
  (*Gnom.* 32, 470)

The state gains more from big souls living in little houses,
  than men with slave mentality living in big houses.
  (*Gnom.* 60, 476)

Your soul is the emanation of god,
  you are his son, esteem this highly.
Don't you know
  that you carry god in yourself?
  (II. 8, 12, 125)

Our goal is to obey the gods,
  so that we may become like god.
  (I. 13)

The soul is like a fortress under siege,
  whose defenders keep vigil behind the walls.

If the foundations are strong,
  the fortress is unconquerable.
    (IV. 5, 25)

If you want to become good,
  first be convinced that you are bad.
    (*Gnom.* 13, 488)

Refrain yourself from evil,
  and deny your evil inclinations.
    (Fragm. 10, 411)

A pure soul with proper principles
  becomes in its acts majestic and unwavering.
    (IV. 11, 8, 389)

In everything, big and small, look to god.
    (II. 19, 31, 174)

Teach men the truth that happiness is not where they are expecting it in their blindness and misery. There is no happiness in strength, because Myro and Ofellius were not happy; there is no happiness in power because the consuls were not happy; not in their sum total because Nero, Sardanapal and Agamemnon groaned, cried, tore their hair out since they all were the slaves of circumstances, fooled by appearances. Happiness is hidden in you, in true freedom, in the lack of all ignoble fear, in perfect self-control, in contentment and peace...

What lofty thoughts from the lips of a pagan slave!

The Power of a Great Goal

Every young man has to resolve to achieve a great goal in life, and not remain a commonplace man. Set yourself a lofty goal, and concentrate with all your might on achieving it. You may not achieve it in a few months or in a few years. You may never achieve it. Never mind! By concentrating your thoughts and planning you are getting closer to the goal that appeared inaccessible at first. If you devote all your energies to achieving a lofty goal, day after day you will discover new forces in yourself never dreamed of before.

The privations survived in the trenches of World War I showed how much men can endure. So if you strive with all your might to achieve a goal, then you will realize what a human soul can accomplish.

For example, you might set the goal of giving up a bad habit, which you recognize as your greatest fault. Or, in your report card last year you had some B's and C's–next year they all will be A's no matter what it will cost. Or, you will learn a foreign language, say French, and you will devote half an hour to studying it every day. And so on.

I would also like for you to set broader, more distant goals. Schoolbooks in England are full of sentences like these:

> "You start your work where millions have left off."
> "There is still room for good workers on the top."
> "The best places in the world are still unfilled."
> "There is still great demand for intelligence and
>   character in the market of life."

I would like every young man to convince himself that he has to become a great man. Become learned, educated, with character, better than the majority. He may not achieve this goal. But he has a better chance of achieving it if he soars high like an eagle towards this goal, rather than flying low like a swallow.

"But then every young man would become arrogant and boastful," you might say. I am not afraid of this. I am quite certain that if his soul is animated by lofty ideals, he can more easily conquer base inclinations and sensual desires.

Many young men slowly disintegrate morally exactly because they have no uplifting goals, lofty ideals to strive for. I completely accept the slogan recommended to young people by Andrew Carnegie (1835-1919), one of the richest yet hard-working Americans: "My place is at the top." Except try to get to the top by hard work and by devoted fulfillment of your duty rather than by pulling strings or by using influential friends.

Of course, there are those who do not study and push forward because they are "humble," "content," and "modest."

Not so fast! Cowardliness is not a virtue and laziness is not humility. True humility makes one say, "I am nothing, by myself I am worth nothing"; immediately adding, "but there is nothing in the world I could not do with the help of God."

Repeat the following beautiful prayer of a saint:

> "My God, my God, I am nothing,
> but what I am is wholly yours."

You will gain a lot of moral strength from saying this prayer.

Energy

There is nothing that impresses young men more than courageous energy. And rightly so! This is one of the most attractive traits of man's will. So what do we call energy?

First, it is not daydreaming. Some young men carry out great deeds–in their thoughts. He entertains his friends by telling about the daring deeds he carried out in his dreams. This is not energy. To solve difficult problems in mathematics, to translate sentences of Livius into good English, struggle against my faults–in other words act rather than dream, that is energy.

Energy is not unthinking impetuosity either, which is the curse of many young men. To jump into danger ("God will help me out"), to answer without thinking, to seek out occasions of sin, to seek out bad company, bad books and bad movies–all this is not energy. To start things and leave them off the next day, this is not energy. To start studying French, but deterred by the difficulties stop it a week later. Then start collecting stamps, but losing interest in three days. To start some sport, train recklessly for two weeks, then losing interest and stop. All this is not energy.

There is an excellent saying:

Look before you leap.

First, face the problem. Consider all aspects. When you see that this is something worth doing, that you have to do it, then do not be deterred any more no matter what persistence, sacrifice, and self-denial will be involved; you will do it because it is your duty to do it–that is energy, that is manly character.

Liberty

There is not another word whose magic enchants youth more than "liberty." To grow freely! To develop freely!

To live free as a bird. This desire is instinctive, and therefore must have been given by the Creator. And if so, there must be a purpose to it. Its purpose cannot be to make the biggest possible noise during class breaks and how to evade disciplinary rules. The purpose of the desire for liberty must be the ability to fight obstacles to their ideal development.

The desire for liberty is meant to protect the development of your soul. So you are not supposed to fight against every rule and constraint (that would be licentiousness, unruliness), only fight against passions, inclinations, and obstacles hindering the development of your character. What helps your development, you should not fight. Just as the grape vines do not fight the stakes which support their growth.

Every instinct left to itself is blind. So is the instinct for liberty, which when not controlled by reason, leads man to destruction. We see often the sad fact that many young men are ruined because of misinterpreted liberty. Instincts that escaped the control of reason make them pursue seeming goods that are really harmful to them, and deter them from arduous things necessary for their harmonic development.

A student writing to his friend expresses the same: "Since my father permitted me to smoke, I stopped smoking. It does not taste good any more." To consider every command and prohibition as an unlawful interference is the distortion of the desire for liberty.

At your age, the height of the strivings of every young man is to become free and independent. But your teachers and parents want the same! So try to understand them and cooperate with them. Alas, many refuse to do that. They suddenly want to be independent rather than purposefully educating themselves to become independent. By independence they mean disorder and freedom from obligations, rather than the internal independence that gives strength and control over dispiritedness, caprice, laziness, and other manifestations of the passions.

So how can you work effectively for your spiritual independence? Do not view the commands of your parents, the rules of your school, your everyday obligations as irritating regulations constraining your liberty which you have to obey only if observed by others; on the contrary, obey others as a means of overcoming your love of comfort, bad moods, eccentricities, superficialities, and untrustworthiness. To view commands and rules this way is to work most effectively on the liberty of your soul. *Deo servire regnare est,* says the Latin proverb: "To serve God is to reign."

The ideal of Catholic education is the harmonic development of both body and soul of the youth. For us, both body and soul are sacred. We received both from the Creator to reach our eternal goal. The human body was made sacred by the Incarnation of God the Son. And some day the body will become partaker of our eternal life. Christianity does not view the body as "evil" or "sinful." And it does not aim to weaken or destroy the body. It aims make the body the obedient servant of eternal goals. The commands of our religion are strict, yet they are not obstacles to our liberty; rather, they help and guarantee that the soul can strive and soar. The grape vine is tied to the stake not to constrain its liberty but to help its growth.

Freedom is the purpose of constraint.
As the vine is bound

To happily stretch up into the air
Instead of crawling in the dust.
  (Weber, *Dreizehnlinden*)

We cannot expect less than the Romans. Read what Juvenalis prescribes:

You should pray for a sound mind in a sound body;
for a stout heart that has no fear of death,
and deems length of days the least of Nature's gifts;
that can endure any kind of toil;
that knows neither wrath nor desire,
and thinks that the woes and hard labours of Hercules
are better than the loves and the banquets and the
down cushions of Sardanapalus.

So: a healthy body, a strong soul ready for toil, self-discipline, unassuming modesty, austerity. Only great souls are capable of this.

Youth with Great Souls

When you read "great soul" do not think of heroes with world-shaking deeds, whose name is known everywhere in the world. Most people never once in their life have an opportunity for heroic deeds. Enthusiastic words about what they would do in an expedition to Antarctica, how they could die for their faith, how they would like to give their life for the Lord Jesus among savages, how at any moment they are willing to shed their blood for their country–such words are of little use in our everyday life, since people will have no opportunity for such sacrifices.

The force of this fiery enthusiasm must be harnessed by the sails of the small everyday duties, and then we can gain a lot from them. If you want to travel on a bus or streetcar, you must have small change: hundred dollar bank notes are of no use there. Similarly, the enthusiasm for becoming a martyr or dying for your country has to be changed into small coins so that you can fulfill the commandments of the Catholic religion and the duties to your country. You are not likely to be expected to die for your faith, or for your country. On the contrary, your religion and your country expect you to live a heroic life. And this is harder! The example of the unfortunate suicides shows that often you need more bravery for life than for death.

During World War I, I served in a military hospital on the front. Once, all the soldiers were receiving inoculation against cholera. You know what I witnessed to my great surprise? Big muscular lads who cared nothing for the biggest hail of bullets on the battlefield started trembling before the injection needle. So the fiery enthusiasm is of little use in everyday life. There are people whose bravery is recklessness and vanity rather than a virtue. They think they are not afraid of death, but they do have a great fear of the trials of life, and this fear turns them into traitors and sinners. In the circus you can admire the death-defying jumps of acrobats, but do you think these same people can resist a little lie to extricate themselves from an unpleasant situation? You need less bravery to swim in the icy Danube River in January than to stick to your high moral principles in a frivolous company. It requires bravery to tell the truth. It requires bravery to remain honest. Persisting in high principles makes youth with great souls.

"You are so selfish!"

It is not exactly a compliment to hear this. What is selfishness? It is disorderly, perverted self-love. Proper self-love is a commandment of God, and an instinct planted in us. It guarantees our survival and urges us to avoid anything that is harmful to us. Selfishness, on the other hand, is only a caricature of proper self-love. A selfish young man believes that he is the center of the universe, that the whole world is made for him, that the intended purpose of every human being in the world is to serve his comfort. He even evaluates the events of world history: are they to his advantage?

The smaller the child, the stronger the influence of his senses, the more selfish he is. Just look at a child of four or five. How he demands everything for himself! He collects everything from the room and puts them in front of himself; nobody else should have anything left for them. We forgive this to such a little one (although it is time to start training him in unselfishness). I do not even get scandalized at a first grader writing home from school in the middle of September: "I already have three good friends, Gyula Róka is my best friend in Latin, László Novák is my best friend in math, and Jóska Waigand is my best friend in Hungarian..." As your intellect develops, you have to realize that the world does not exist for you alone, you are not the most important person in the whole world, there are millions of people around you and you have to give them consideration. Whoever does not realize this is called selfish.

It is surprising that boys very easily become selfish exactly during puberty, in the teenage years, when they are usually most proud of their mind, their knowledge. If at home he is insufferable, irritable, annoys his parents, brothers and sisters, slams doors, peevish, always unsatisfied, has no consideration for anybody, they say "Poor thing, he is nervous!" when in fact they should say, "Poor thing, he is selfish!" It is selfishness when a well-to-do boy talks about his wonderful vacation trip to a poor classmate. It is selfishness to let a swinging door go when someone is behind you. It is selfishness to laugh in a family that has a sorrow. It is selfishness to tease and annoy others.

You have to start practicing unselfishness at a young age. It is selfishness to seek only your own success, and trample down others to accomplish it. But how did you get to that stage? You started in childhood with insignificant things. When walking in the woods, you went in front of others, pushed the branches aside and then let the branches slam into the faces of those that followed.

On the other hand, what an honor to be called a generous young man! Generosity is the opposite of selfishness. If your classmate suffered a setback, console him with a few heartfelt words, this is generosity. If he rejoices over something, rejoice with him; this is generosity (the selfish would be full of envy). If you share your lunch with your poor classmate, you are generous. If you help your classmate in studying, if you are attentive and give pleasure to others, if you treat hired help with respect and consideration, if you pick up an object dropped by somebody, you are unselfish. So, you see it is possible to fill even a student's life with noble-minded details and fraternal charity.

Can You Say No?

Every young man of character must be able to say No! When the passions are stirred up, when you have been insulted and are tempted to a sharp retort that would drag you into sin, are you then able to say the decisive word: No! There will be no explosion, there will be no fight, there will be no arguing! Caesar controlled his rash and hasty speech by counting up to twenty before answering. An excellent means to help our better self, our consideration to regain control.

A young man is skiing on a beautiful snow-covered slope. A precipice is awaiting him just around the corner. He is flying like an arrow, yet comes to a sudden halt with a swift uphill turn and stands there like a granite column. Bravo! Where did you learn it? Well, I started by learning how to stop on gentler slopes. Life is like a ski trail full of hazards. Many will fall into the precipices and perish, unless they learn to stop dead before them, and learn to say NO to the storm of passions. Training the will is nothing but the systematic support of the soul in its fight against the nearly irresistible rule of the body. If one gives in to all impulses without any resistance, his soul will be in a frightening chaos. Now we understand the words of Our Lord:

> The kingdom of heaven suffereth
>   violence,
> and the violent bear it away.
>   (Matt. 11:12)

The first requirement of character: struggle against ourselves, using violence against our perverse inclinations to force order on the jungle of our disordered instinctive forces.

In the First World War the slogan "attack is the best defense" was much used. Indeed, whoever attacks first obtains many advantages. So in the battle for your soul you also have to attack relentlessly the hostile army of passions inside you: laziness, love of comfort, lack of charity, caprice, gluttony, curiosity, *etc.*

> Whoever has not learned
> to deny himself in his youth,
> Who always gratifies his desires,
> Is his own worst enemy.
> He hurts himself by word and deed,
> And kills himself before his time.
> (Weber)

I fear you may not be willing to believe what incredible self-control was manifested by Firmin Abauzit (1679-1767), a French scholar in Geneva. For twenty-two years he measured and recorded barometric pressure every day. One day a new servant was hired, who immediately carried out a thorough house cleaning. The scholar asks the servant: "Where are all those papers that were lying next to the barometer?" "Those dirty papers, sir? I threw them into the fire, and replaced them with brand new and clean ones." What would you have said? Abauzit folded his arms (it was obvious that a great storm was raging in his soul) and said quietly: "You have destroyed the results of my work of twenty-two years. Do not touch anything else in this room ever." See if you could remain this calm even in much less important matters.

Do you know why so many young men smoke? (even if they know it is a harmful passion). Because it tastes good? No. Rather because others smoke too. Why do they criticize everything so loudly? Because others do it. Why are they frivolous? Because others are like that.

It takes great strength of mind to dare to defend your moral principles in a company that is opposed to them. It takes impressive courage not to yield your religious convictions for the sake of anybody. But if you do not have this courage, your character is still weak, you are not yet a young man of character.

There are so many young men who would bravely charge into battle, but at a party they are ashamed of confessing their faith because "what would people say." There are many who despite their noble moral principles merely giggle when they hear some indecent talk, and they even join in "because others do the same." A person of character does not say: "The way he talks is the way I shall talk." A person of character does not say: "The way he acts is the way I shall act." The flower opens its petals to the morning sun; it is not interested in what the other flowers do, but basks in the warm sunshine. Face the sun! says the young man of character. The eagle is not watching what the other birds do, whether they will also fly with him, but takes off and soars into the great heights towards the sun. Upwards, *ad astra*, to the stars, should be the slogan of the young man of character.

It is a great blessing to be able to say NO when necessary. Say NO to your companions when they are trying to talk you into something forbidden. Say NO to your instincts when they are making their blind demands. Say NO to every temptation that tries to entangle you.

From a Diary

The following are taken from the diary of a fifth-grade student in Budapest. One of the actors is frivolously swimming with the tide, the other has character and can say No.

"Yesterday I went to visit Peczkai, although I do not think I shall visit him again. Schöpfer encouraged me to go, although I have always had an aversion to Peczkai. Especially when he once said after religion class: 'This is not for grown-ups, this is for children.'

"First I have to write about his room, as disordered as a flea market. I rang the bell. A manservant in uniform opened the door: 'The young gentleman is studying in his room. This way, please...' In the rooms there are many indications of wealth, they are expensively furnished with Persian rugs and large paintings. I knock on the door of the 'young gentleman' but he must be studying very hard because there is no answer. I open the door quietly. Peczkai is sleeping over a magazine. Under it is a French grammar book, to be switched quickly in case Dad is approaching. This time he would have gotten into trouble...

"Before awakening the diligent student, I look around the room. On the desk, there is a soccer ball with ink poured on it, a bicycle pump, half a glove, a ruler, an eraser, various buttons, and a math book. On the other side a screwdriver, a lighter, half of a Latin dictionary (the other half is under the desk). Blotting pad, 50-60 foreign stamps, skate key, cuff links. Many books, the Hungarian novels of Mikszáth mixed with mystery stories, algebra and German books. On top of it all Peczkai is peacefully asleep. (Is he this disordered inside?)

"Suddenly he wakes up. Automatically reaches for the French grammar to switch with the magazine, but when he realizes it is not his Dad who came in, he offers his hand: 'Oh, it is you. Hello, please take a seat. Have some cigarettes, real Egyptian' and pulls out a lot of cigarettes from the desk.

"'Thank you, I do not smoke. Where did you get the cigarettes from?'

"'From my Dad. You don't smoke? Oh, you are a child who does not break the rules.'

"I started boiling inside, but answered calmly: 'It is true I do not do what my parents forbid. I always realize that they are right. But it is also my principle not to smoke, and I stick to my principles.' Then he started talking about his vacations at Lake Balaton and about his motorcycle. Also talked about various silly things slowly edging into indecent jokes, even though he could see that they got a very cool reception from me. Finally, when he fished out from his books photos of scantily dressed actresses, and launched into the stories of his conquests, I stood up and left.

"I was engulfed in seething anger, and it took considerable self-control to merely say in parting: 'I believed that you invited me to a more civilized entertainment.' After this disappointing visit I had to go out to the riverbank. Some unexplainable force drove me to the

Danube, seeking fresh air and the clear night. It was a winter night, the stars sparkled in the cold sky. It was a lonely walk, my troubled soul crying to the sky as if praying: Oh, stars, how pure you are, sparkling and spotless! And how soiled this world is, and how soiled many souls in it! I wandered around for a long time meditating on purity. This was my first visit to Peczkai, and I am quite certain that it will be my last..."

Kite on the Telegraph Wire

Every virtue is based on self-control. Once one becomes the slave of his passions, he loses the chief guarantee of his moral life: the ability to command himself. The one in the grip of sensual desires with no resistance offered not only has no character, he is not human any more. The concept of "man" includes the ability to command, the ability to resist the unrestrained, lawless demands of the body. It is astonishing to find in life that not only children, who are after all under the overwhelming control of the senses, but also grown-ups act impulsively. Their self-control is unbelievably weak, and thus they are not able to consider whether their act is correct, justified, or desirable, and what will be its consequences. They are driven by waves of hurt vanity, anger, sensuality, and pride into acts that they will truly regret in five minutes. The vast majority of sins would disappear from the world if people would learn one thing: to command themselves.

The pagan philosopher Crates was once slapped in the face so hard by the painter Nicodromus that his face became swollen. Do you know how Crates retaliated? You might think: he hit back! No. He placed a sign on his swollen face: "Done by Nicodromus!" So that everybody could see the weakness of Nicodromus.

> He who trusts his life to chance,
> Who does not adhere to self-discipline,
> Always remains life's slave.
> (Goethe)

One of my students handled a similar incident differently. He accidentally bumped into his classmate, who immediately responded with "You are the greatest idiot in the world!" My student answered quietly: "Sorry, but how can you forget yourself so?"

It is said that people today are very materialistic. Indeed, it is sad but true. Yet even these materialistic people admire deeply spirit conquering matter. A few years ago the whole world enthusiastically received the news that Amundsen (1872-1928), the Norwegian explorer of polar regions, after many privations and trials had finally reached the South Pole! And there was deep sympathy on receiving the news that Shackleton (1874-1922), the Anglo-Irish explorer of polar regions, died suddenly. Why are these explorers celebrated? They have not opened new diamond mines, they have not constructed new machines. They are celebrated because in them the human spirit conquers the forces of matter, of body and of nature.

Read how Hédervári Kont and his thirty companions behaved before the tyrant (according to folk legends, they were executed in 1393 in Buda by Zsigmond, King of Hungary), and follow their example when you have to resist the unlawful demands of your fallen human nature:

> In my hand is life and death,
> You hear, rebels?
> Who kneels receives life–
> But nobody moves.
> They all are men and heroes,
> True patriots,
> To shed their blood
> They are not afraid.
>   (Garay, *Kont*)

In a small country town once I met a little boy crying bitterly. He worked on a kite for days, decorated it beautifully, but when trying to fly it, it got stuck in a telegraph wire. The beautiful kite fluttered powerlessly on the wire, tearing more and more, as the boy watched his hard work falling to pieces.

Similarly, the soul of every young man would also soar upwards, but, alas, it is often struck down and is writhing on the rocks of temptations and doubt, in the web of passions, and remains arrested there. Poor little boy, how he cries when his kite that started soaring gets entangled in the telegraph wire and is there destroyed. Take care that your soul wanting to soar does not similarly get arrested in the claws of passions and in the jungle of instinctive forces.

Contra Torrentem!

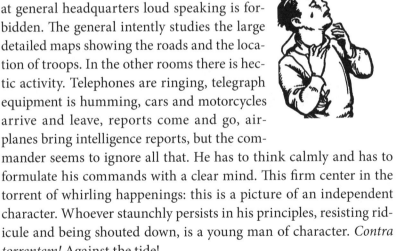

Imagine the commanding general in a great war, how he plans his actions and decides the fate of hundreds of thousands. In his room at general headquarters loud speaking is forbidden. The general intently studies the large detailed maps showing the roads and the location of troops. In the other rooms there is hectic activity. Telephones are ringing, telegraph equipment is humming, cars and motorcycles arrive and leave, reports come and go, airplanes bring intelligence reports, but the commander seems to ignore all that. He has to think calmly and has to formulate his commands with a clear mind. This firm center in the torrent of whirling happenings: this is a picture of an independent character. Whoever staunchly persists in his principles, resisting ridicule and being shouted down, is a young man of character. *Contra torrentem!* Against the tide!

If one always asks: what will people say? he is a slave of human respect, he is not yet an independent character. Daniel was fourteen years old when captured by Nabuchodonosor, and was kept in the royal court. You can imagine what luxury, splendor, and temptations surrounded him. And his reaction? "I will remain faithful to my God and will not eat of the forbidden meat." This lasted for three years, and he remained faithful among the temptations of the royal palace. He was a young man of character!

A university student wrote about the First World War: "I think I have landed among the worst. I am totally alone, without friends who would think like me... These are jolly fellows, but they turn everything into evil. They distort the songs, and insert unthinkable things into them. They read books aloud containing the most indecent things described in great detail. I have to listen to things I have never even dreamed about. The loudest of them is a volunteer, who always uses his little knowledge for evil. Whenever possible, I disappeared from the room. But sometimes this was not possible. When we were all at table, he started his indecent talk. I tried to occupy myself with other things and tried not to listen. But then they forced me to. And from then on everybody targeted me. They punished me, I had to do all the menial jobs. I was ready to complain when they moved me to another unit. So at last I am free, and I am not forced to listen to vile things." This is a heroic young man, an independent character. Dares to go against the tide. *Contra torrentem!*

Under communism (of 1919) it was forbidden to pray before classes. "Comrade teacher" enters one of the classrooms of a Budapest school and tells the class to sit down. They remain standing. "What is the matter? Sit down!" The boys answer in unison: "We have not yet prayed." The comrade is livid: "You know it is forbidden to pray." The boys repeat in unison: "We have not yet prayed." "Well, then pray!" the comrade gave up. These boys were heroic.

The man with a strong will is like a waterfall, he prepares his way even among rocks. And the brave, independent characters stand out like pyramids from the dishonorable barren desert of the modern world.

Most likely it will not be given to you to perform great heroic deeds in your entire life. But your life can still be exemplary and heroic, if you perform the small duties of every day life diligently and faithfully.

Just do not be afraid of the loudmouths! If you courageously speak up for your principles, you will often see that your opponent will back down. He is not a wild bull ready to gore you; rather, he is a snail ready to withdraw his tentacles at the first touch.

We are happy to find that the youth of today has more religion that the one of twenty or thirty years ago. Otherwise, European culture would disappear. Rabindranath Tagore (1861-1941), the great poet of India, during his travels through Europe concluded that the morals of the so-called Christian Europe are below the morals of the pagan East. The materialist spirit of the nineteenth century, denying soul, ideals, God, and eternal life, pushed Western culture into a fatal decline, and there is no power able to prevent its destruction except a consistently religious youth able to have zeal for noble ideals. Consistently religious youth! That is to say, Catholic not only according to the register of births, but daring to be Catholic in his whole life too. Every one of his acts and thoughts is the consequence of the assertion: I am a Catholic young man! I live consistently like a Catholic, now as a student, and also later out in life. Always and everywhere corresponding to my religious convictions!

Duel

"Please be careful, consider who you are dealing with. Since six minutes ago I am also qualified for dueling...," asserts a young man who has just graduated from high school, and who has just been

bumped on the stairs by one of his classmates. He said it very seriously, not realizing that he is just one of those swimming with the
tide. His seriousness contained all the perverted views and mistaken
thinking used by today's society to defend the honor of persons. It
will be useful for you to read a few thoughts about this. We can hear
it from the best of young men: "It is true that dueling is foolish. It is a
primitive way of serving justice left to us from the past. But no matter,
it is unavoidable in certain cases. In certain cases I cannot get myself
satisfaction in any other way."

So that is it. The purpose of dueling is to get satisfaction. If somebody lied, cheated, violated someone's honor, and I tell him that to
his face, what right does he have to demand satisfaction? He should
repent and change his ways, that is the way for him to get his honor
back. Does drawing a sword or a pistol prove that he is an honest
man? The only thing he proved is that he is willing to risk his life carelessly. Every burglar, murderer, acrobat, and lion tamer does the same.

Consider calmly this matter, and you will realize that a duel is
completely inadequate to give satisfaction. A duel may have three
possible outcomes: Both parties get injured–in this case who received
satisfaction? If the innocent party receives injury, where is the satisfaction? And finally, it is possible that the challenger gets injured,
or may even die. What does that mean? We moderns are proud to
say: we all are equal before the law. But just consider: if two peasant
boys knife each other while drunk, they get a jail sentence of several
months although they were morally irresponsible. At the same time,
if two gentlemen, after training for several days, cut each other in cold
blood, they get three days in jail. Where is the "equality" of the twentieth century here? Isn't your sense of justice offended? You hear the
complaint: people have lost respect for the law. But how can the lower
classes respect the law when the upper classes are not penalized for
violating the law. I would like you, my son, to resist dueling when you
grow up. Dueling is not required for character.

I know that many serious people who condemn dueling on religious grounds still say that in certain cases, as a result of "societal
pressures," they cannot evade dueling. They are completely wrong.

Honor consists in the moral perfection of a person; one can lose his honor by his own deeds. It is a completely pagan idea that honor can be lost as a result of an abuse or insult coming from the outside. The noble Romans did not duel but turned to the courts, yet they were not cowards!

"Honor and courage are noble virtues of the soul which cannot be acquired by weapons, and lack of honor and cowardice are flaws of the soul which blood cannot wash away" (János Csernoch, Prince Primate of Hungary, 1912-1927).

I admit that the unfortunate perception still exists that insults and injuries should be righted, not through laws, but should be avenged through the very inadequate means of dueling. I also admit that superficial judgment may still label someone a coward who refuses to duel; all the more we need courageous men with impressive characters who dare to break with this custom. I happen to know well-known personalities who openly proclaim that they would never duel because of their religious convictions and yet they are surrounded by the greatest respect. Of course, it is their strictest rule not to offend anybody. Because to offend others and then evade giving satisfaction is not Christianity but cowardice. If you happen to have been rash, after all we are all human, it takes more courage to admit our mistake and ask for forgiveness than to duel. Dueling is a self-help left for us from earlier ages when man had to fight to get some justice for himself. In our civilized world one should not administer justice for himself. Work therefore by setting an example so that dueling would disappear from the world just as blood feuds also disappeared. It is not worthy of a courageous youth to suppress his noble principles for the sake of the barbarism of a social class.

Recently I have heard about a young man who fought a duel just after high school graduation. They had a disagreement in the sixth grade and nurtured their dislike of each other until finally the great day has arrived when they became "capable of dueling." My God! Such immature kids come out of high school?

Yes, a Hungarian young man will gladly sacrifice his life and blood for the sake of truth, country, religion and great ideas, but not for the sake of stupid public opinion. Dueling is a sin against God, a sin against yourself and a sin against your fellow man, and a great folly in itself. You see, the Catholic Church displayed great courage by having fought for centuries against this foolishness, excommunicated those dueling and their seconds, resisted public opinion, and will not yield until people change. We smile over the Middle Ages when witches were burned. In the future, people will smile over men who were cutting each other with swords "to save their honor."

The most important question is: what can you do against dueling? To make it disappear? One man cannot accomplish that. But you can still accomplish a lot. Respect the honor of others so that there is no need for dueling. If your words and behavior do not give others the necessary respect, you will find yourself involved in a duel. Do not allow others to be slandered and calumniated in your presence, and you have prevented many duels. If your friend had a disagreement with somebody, smooth the matter over without duel (most duels are caused by the seconds). If dueling is discussed, do not hide your conviction that you do not consider it a means to defend honor, and that you are not convinced that behind a face cut with a sword there is necessarily an honest soul. The hero is not the one winning a duel, the hero is the one conquering himself. You read it on a tombstone: *Victor hostium et sui*. Four words, and an incredible compliment. "He conquered the enemy, and he conquered himself." Many have done the first, few have done the second.

"*Victor Hostium et Sui*"

There is hardly a more difficult task than to convince a young man of fourteen or sixteen years about the sublimity of self-control, calmness, and patience. If my friend trips me up, I angrily punch him in return; if someone attacks me, I hit him over the head; if someone makes fun of me, I tell him off–such things are hard to resist. It is even harder to believe that refusing to do them is neither cowardice nor shyness, but an expression of manly willpower! Yet it is true!

So Goethe is right:

Restraint will prove the master,
Only the law can give us freedom.

Self-control is not merely silence and passive resignation, but a manifestation of disciplined will, which remains in control in all circumstances able to weigh the significance of every word uttered. Self-control is unattractive to youth because it is misunderstood. It does not mean tolerating every attack with sheepish imbecility, leaving insults unanswered. Not at all! Attacks should be answered not by lowering ourselves by outbursts and violence to the level of the attacker; rather, by our dignified manner and carefully chosen words we should hit the most vulnerable point of the attacker. If you do not have self-control, you are like one who cannot walk, you barely stand on your feet, and you stumble into everybody. Without self-control you cannot have character. Our Lord Jesus Christ gave a beautiful example of manly self-control when during his trial a soldier struck him on the face. He could have punished the insult with death. Instead, what did He do?

He said with superhuman calm:

If I have spoken evil,
    give testimony of the evil;
    but if well, why strikest thou me?
    (John 18:23)

Fort or Weather Vane?

In medieval towns one can often see remnants of old fortresses. Even if most of it is in ruins, a tower still stubbornly resists the erosion of time. When these ancient towers like immovable rocks look down into the whirlwind of new life they appear to be the embodiment of character: around them everything is changing, bending, adapting, but they themselves do not compromise their principles.

This tower is the symbol of a strong character, the symbol of a man doing his duty. Just as in olden times the tower was the strongest defense of the inhabitants of the castle, now the man of character is the strongest pillar of human society. Where your calling has placed you, that is where you stay like a man, says the ancient tower. See, I have not been built in one day, I have been built from so many little bricks and stones, with a lot of exertion, with a lot of good will, with a lot of sweat, but now here I stand unshakeable.

It is easy for our good will to slacken and wane. You often start out enthusiastically: I will start traveling the road to character, I will work hard at it, and then in just a few hours, a few days, the enthusiasm cools off, and you remained unchanged. The tower of the fort was built over years or decades, and you want to build your character in

a day? But consider: the road of sin appears pleasant at first but leads to a terrible awakening; following virtue is very hard at first, but gets easier with each step, and leads to the peace of a good conscience.

But there is something on the top of the tower, something turning this way and that way–a weather vane. It has no fixed direction, it has no firm foundation; I might even say: it has no principles, it has no character. If it had, the wind would be blowing in vain. To give up principles, to compromise convictions because it is more comfortable that way, because it will result in a better career in the world that way, because the wind is blowing that way: that is the nature of the weather vane. But do tell me, is he a man if his deeds, principles, and convictions are dictated by external circumstances and human opinions? Yet, how many such young men do you know? These are the ones who cannot stand on their own feet, who are still intellectually minors, who always ask what their neighbor might say?

His conscience says: Do not read that book, it is full of immoral filth. All right, I will not read it then. Then comes his friend: Oh, you are still a child. What? Me a child? And proceeds to read the book. And tramples his innocent soul into the mud.

His conscience says: Do not go to that play or movie, or quit that bad company. Yes, but all the others go, and all the others have a good time. Why do I have to be the exception? This is the way the weather vane thinks and acts. So which one do you want to be? Fort or weather vane? A captive of a cowardly fear of men, or a captive of your own conscience?

A Captive of Conscience

A captive of conscience. It sounds like the title of a mystery story, you may think. Wrong. The greatest compliment we can give a young man is to say: He is lord of his will and captive of his conscience. Consistently and uncompromisingly faithful to the dictates of your conscience: if you are capable of this, you are a young man of character.

Every wagon has a small nail in it, barely noticeable: the linchpin. It is a locking pin inserted in the end of the axle to prevent the wheel from slipping off. If it falls out, the wagon goes on for a while more, then the wheel slips off and the wagon turns over. On the path of virtue you can find a comparable little thing. It is unconditional adherence to the word of your conscience. So be an obedient servant of your conscience.

There are two enemies fighting against your conscience. The whole world around you speaks against it; and your disordered inclinations and awakening instincts entice you to folly.

Once in a while you have ardent moments, you seem to have left the earth and soar in the pure heights. You are determined always to follow your conscience. You will never deviate from the road of honor. You will never commit sin, in thought, word or deed. You feel happy, good and light. And what next? This mate of yours or that does not keep God's commandments. Your noble principles are ridiculed in this book or in that play or movie. And then comes the hardest trial! If the whole world is bad, can you remain good? If the whole school consists of dishonorable boys, can you still remain faithful to your noble principles? If everybody is lying, but you, never! If all the boys miss their Sunday Mass, but you, never! If their language is filthy, but yours, never!

Then there comes yet another trial. There is an enemy not on the outside, but on the inside, in your own being. Conscience is called the word of God, and justly. Who has not heard it? When he was tempted to fight, a warning was heard like a little bell: Don't do it! Don't do it! When he was tempted to take something belonging to another he again heard the warning. And when he encountered an even more serious temptation, the warning bell was loudly crying: Don't do it! Don't do it!

I ask you again, my son, to train yourself in your youth to listen to the voice of your conscience unconditionally. This will determine whether you will become a conscientious man. The conscientious man is the pillar of society on whom everything rests.

> A man's word is good protection,
> A man's action is better advice.
> The best protection and advice
> Is a man of his word and deed.
> (Rückert)

Whoever is the captive of his conscience, he is the captive of God, and being a captive of God is the greatest freedom. I cannot imagine a greater compliment than the one received by an English MP who died young: the Ten Commandments stamped His whole being.

Be afraid of nothing except your conscience! It is not upright to abandon anything that your conscience prescribes because you are afraid that others will disparage or ridicule you. If you are afraid of praying openly or of genuflecting in church because "others will see it" you are not a captive of your own conscience, but a captive of a cowardly fear of men. Aldous Huxley (1894-1963) was right when he wrote: "True manliness means strong will guided by a gentle conscience." You have no will power and your character is undeveloped if you always fearfully watch what others might say. And you have no strong character if you follow your heart but ignore your intellect, if you prefer pleasant desires to strict duty.

> Don't ask your heart what it desires,
> Ask your conscience about your duty.
> (F. W. Weber)

The Persian rulers tried to guarantee a good sleep for themselves by hiding several talents of gold (representing a huge amount of money) in their pillow. The Roman emperor Caligula added wild animals to his palace guard to make sure nobody disturbed his rest. Artemon placed a large shield over his head for protection in case the building should collapse. All for nothing! The best way to guarantee a good sleep is to have a good conscience:

> A good conscience is the gentlest pillow to sleep on.

Be the ruler of your will and captive of your conscience!

Saint Peter of Verona (Saint Peter Martyr) was killed with a dagger. After the first stabs he cried: "Credo! I believe!" When he could not speak any more, he dipped his fingers in his own blood and wrote on the ground: "Credo!" He was a man of character, a captive of his own conscience.

CHAPTER TWO

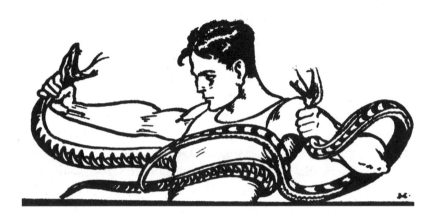

Obstacles to Character Formation

There are many obstacles to building our character, and if you stumble over them your character will be ruined.

One obstacle to the development of character is the constant worrying: Well, all right, I do have this firm principle in this matter, but if I follow it, what are people going to say? If you always try to please people and are ready to deny your principles for their sake, you can never become a firm character. A young man of character never cares about what people will say about his actions, rather what his conscience will say about the same. It is a deplorable situation when a young man, "for the sake of society" (or rather for the fear of men), speaks or acts in a manner that his conscience rejects.

Another obstacle to building character is the jungle of unregulated passions inside us. Every young man has a dominant fault: recognizing it and correcting it is the surest way to character formation. Do not waste your time with the extermination of small, insignificant faults. Tackle the dominant one, the others will be easily taken care of.

In one boy the dominant fault might be love of comfort which makes all work repugnant; in the second, gluttony; in the third, gossiping; in the fourth, sudden anger, exaggerated self-confidence or stubbornness, *etc.* All these are rebels in the realm of your soul that must be chained.

The most dangerous obstacle to forming character is its slowness. Self-education is a work of years or decades.

Have you studied crystallization? If so, you know that if we place into a saturated solution of various materials a seed crystal, a small piece of single crystal material, then slowly the like molecules will be drawn together. The crystal slowly begins to grow, and if nothing disturbs the process a beautiful large crystal of the same material will be grown. Disturbances result in small, imperfect, or distorted crystals.

There is a similar process of crystallization in human souls also. If you plant noble ideals in your soul as "seed crystals" they draw together other similar ideals, and if this state persists throughout your youth, the good in you will develop into a beautiful crystal. But in the "saturated solution" of the human soul there are many molecules of moral evil too. If a young man disturbs this crystallization process with his moral failures, the moral failures draw the molecules of moral evil together, and the soul of the young man becomes a distorted crystal.

Leaves in the Whirlwind

A great obstacle to character formation is the hectic pace of modern life, the mad rush and millions of conflicting impressions which do not favor the quiet development of character. Happy is the young man who can devote some time to the development of his soul, and still can find time in his evening prayer to descend into his own soul to find sediments of sin there. Whoever swims with the tide carelessly will never know himself. A situation to be pitied: a young man may know the state of Alaska, may be able to list the tributaries of the Yangtze River, yet does not know his own soul! If he knew it, he would be terrified of that jungle inhabited by the wild beasts of uncontrolled passion. Such young men will never become independent even when they grow up; rather, they are tossed by lowly material interests, human considerations, and passions just as the lifeless yellow leaves are tossed by the November wind. Leaves in the whirlwind!

Such young men will, even when they grow up, be like a piece of wood in the torrents of a river going, not knowing where or why. Like sheep mindlessly following the bellwether, not knowing where or why. Like the weather vane turning this way and that, not knowing why. Leaves in the whirlwind!

The Iron Cross

In the First World War a large Russian force encircled a small group of German soldiers and forced them to retreat to a small hut. There was no doubt about the eventual outcome of the engagement. The Russians demanded surrender, the response was heavy fire from the hut. The Russians shelled the hut until the German fire died out; they ran out of ammunition. The Russians enter the hut, and find most Germans dead. The German commander, Lieutenant Griesheim is also dying. The Russians, not the enemy any more but sympathetic comrades, ask: "You have seen our superiority, why did you not surrender?" With a great effort Lieutenant Griesheim answers pointing to his chest: "Whoever wears this, does not surrender." On his chest was the Iron Cross...

My dear son, when you encounter heavy obstacles on the road to character, you also should think of the cross you received at your baptism from Our Lord, and say often:

> The world may gleam, delights allure,
> Coax and sing and joke,
> We carry the victorious cross on our chest,
> And the ardor of the cross in our heart.
> (Eichert)

Cockle in the Harvest

Look at the wheat field in May! Among the fresh crops you see cockle, weedy plants appearing. They are still small, still look harmless, but as they grow, they become more and more prickly, hard, and coarse. My son, you are living the May of your life, and you can also notice in the harvest of your soul cockle springing up. In your childhood, your faults, naughtiness, stubbornness were not very dangerous, but as you grow, all your faults are becoming more and more prickly and coarse, and you have to start fighting them.

What happens to the boy who does not do the fighting because he does not care about his soul? His legs are getting longer and longer, his lungs are getting larger and larger, but his soul gets ignored. What will happen to him? The cockle, the weeds, will grow vigorously (not only does it not need any care, it likes to grow in neglected earth), whereas the wheat will waste away and die out. Such a young man when told to do something responds with ugly faces. When asked a question, he shrugs his shoulders angrily. When he does not like something, he slams the door. His shoelace breaks, he swears loudly. Somebody bumps into him during play, he responds with a slap in the face. If he meets a weaker one, immediately he picks a fight with him. In other words, he becomes an insufferable teenager. Poor thing!

With the same effort he could have become a young man of character had he started to fight the cockles in time.

Take care! There are cockles in every soul. In yours too. The wise young man does not allow them to grow, but weeds them out with great effort. This is what we call self-education.

The Struggle in the Soul

There is a constant struggle in the soul between good and evil. In the early years (childhood and youth) this struggle is especially strong, later it subsides somewhat, but never comes to an end. Who is struggling in us, and against whom?

You were barely five or six years old when you felt the first appearance of the enemy. You felt that there is something in you pulling you towards evil. Something like a lead weight pulling you towards the deep, towards the bottomless pit of moral evil. Some terrible inheritance, which our Faith considers the consequence of Original Sin, and calls inclination to do evil. This is very useful to know. To know that man is more inclined to do evil than to do good. But you have experienced this many times. There are so many obstacles in the way to the ideal development of our soul. We know the noble ideals Our Lord Jesus Christ set before us: let us strive to live according to them. But, alas, I also notice a tragic division in me. The good appeals to me, but sin entices me. The ideal life draws me upwards, sin pulls me downwards. I would like to soar towards the heights of ideal life, but temptations are weighing on me like lead. You must have felt manifestations of the great battle that a little schoolboy expressed in this way: "Please, sir, why is it that it is so good to be bad, and so bad to be good?"

Whoever wins in this battle is the real hero. The boy ready for a fist fight any minute is not the hero. The hero is the one who can control himself, his evil inclinations. The hero is the one who turns away from immoral pictures, dirt and filth instantaneously. The hero is the one able to ask for forgiveness immediately after having given offense. The hero is the one who sticks with his honorable principles even in the middle of temptations.

And without Sacrifices?

All this is wonderful. To have character! I also want that! To live an upright life! I also strive for that. But isn't there an easier way? Is there only one way to character? Couldn't it be obtained somehow more cheaply, without sacrifices? No, the price cannot be reduced. Our Lord says it Himself: "If any man will come after me, let him deny himself, and take up his cross, and follow me" (Matt. 16:24).

If you want to enter heaven with Him, you must not abandon Him on the way to Calvary either. But what can you obtain in this world "for free"? Nothing, absolutely nothing. Just look and see how people are killing themselves, working day and night, for perishable things. And you would like to acquire this great treasure, your character, without work? "Oh, how easy you have it!" says a young man when he finds his friend in the middle of some revelry. How good it must be to be a happy-go-lucky person! How much joy there must be in constant dancing and partying...

You are quite wrong, my son. If you could look into the heart that is constantly pursuing worldly pleasures, what would you see there? Not joy and satisfaction, but emptiness and forced smiles.

Holy Scripture is right:

> But the wicked are like the raging sea, which cannot rest,
>   and the waves thereof cast up dirt and mire.
> (Is. 57:20)

He is tossed restlessly in the storm of passions, and is sad when the storm quiets down. Read what John Stuart Mill (1806-1873) says about this: If someone never denies himself something permitted, he certainly cannot be expected to give up forbidden things. No doubt the time will come when children will be systematically taught asceticism and self-denial, just like in ancient times, to deny their desires, to defy dangers, and to suffer pains voluntarily.

This is the reason the Catholic religion prescribes self-denial, the training of the will and asceticism. Asceticism? "Horrors!" you think, because you have been wrongly convinced that asceticism means austerities and the killing of the joys of human life. The original meaning of this word is "fine finish": the Greeks meant the training and disciplined life with which a competitor prepared himself for a sporting event to bring the maximum out of his body.

Character is also the result of training, striving, and competition. The fine finish of ourselves cannot be done without training, and so our holy religion prescribes exercises of self-denial exactly to help us develop our character. There is no worldly success without sacrifices and self-denial, and yet you expect to develop your character in the middle of comfort and ease?

You must know that when one is preparing for a sports competition, his training has two thrusts. Say he will take part in a rowing competition. He gets up early in the morning. He goes out to the rowing club. He gets into the boat and rows and sweats every day for three hours, just to start it all over again next day, then on the third day again for many weeks. The other side of his training is to live an austere life, refrain himself from most pleasures. He eats little bread, pasta, and baked goods so as not to gain weight. He must not smoke. No alcoholic drinks. Every day he goes to sleep early, *etc., etc.* And all this is for the sake of a little medal and the glory of being first. And you do not want to make an effort for your character?

Another thought: everybody makes sacrifices in life, except different people make sacrifices for different things. Have you seen the avaricious, the miserly? How destitute he is; how he scrapes together penny by penny his money. He barely eats, he wears rags, he does not go for walks so as not to wear down his shoes, he lives without friends. All that for what? To scrape together some wealth. He sacrifices his personality, his joys, his honor for money. Isn't it worth making sacrifices for much nobler goals?

Look at the greedy. He rushes to and fro, he greatly exerts himself, he has not a minute's rest. Why? Again for money. Look at the vainglorious! He recklessly risks his life to gain fame. Another spends whole nights dancing. If he made just half of that effort to help his fellow man!

The French Dominican Lacordaire (1802-1861) said: "In every man hides a saint and a criminal." The criminal will grow without any attention, but it will take a lot of hard work and self-education to make sure that the saint will dominate. It will not happen without a struggle. The sculptor has to cut a great deal with a chisel from the large block of marble, and you will have to whittle a lot if you want to shape your own soul. A beautiful sculpture takes a lot of time, and a character even more so. Deliberate and persevering efforts are needed! Adopt the motto of Charles V (1500-1558), Holy Roman Emperor: *Plus! Ultra!* Yet more! Yet farther! The Greek painter Zeuxis (fifth century B.C.) was asked why he worked on his pictures with such diligence? "Because I work for eternity" was the answer.

My son, you really work for eternity when you work on your soul. Do not think it requires too much work.

The Animal Tamer Monk

Many boys would be willing to kill a dragon in the forest like Siegfried, the legendary dragon-slaying hero, but they have no patience to fight against the dragons of their own evil inclinations. Yet that work is such a blessed effort!

One evening the abbot of an old monastery asked one of his monks: "What have you worked on today?" "Oh, I had so much to do today, just as every day, that I got through it all only by the grace of God. Every day I have to guard two falcons, hold back two deer, compel two hawks, hold a worm in check, restrain a bear, and nurse and protect a patient."

"What are you saying?" laughed the abbot. "There is no such work in our monastery."

"Oh, yes, there is," answered the monk.

"The two falcons are my two eyes: I have to guard them lest they look at sinful things. The two deer are my legs: I have to hold them back lest they lead me into sin. The two hawks are my hands: I have to compel them to work and to do good deeds. The worm is my tongue: I have to hold it in check so as not to speak in a vain and sinful manner.

The bear is my heart: I have to restrain it from self-love and vanity. And the patient is my whole body: I have to protect it so that sensuality does not conquer it."

Our fight against the disordered passions is like the work of an animal tamer, and this work must be done every day without stopping if we want to develop a character. The young man serious about character will never excuse himself by saying, "Well, it cannot be helped; this is my nature, I was born this way." Rather, he will work on perfecting his soul. Say to yourself: Even if there are wild beasts in me, I shall tame them! I shall become what I want to be, rather than remain the way I was born!

In the words of Sebastian Sailer (1714-1777):

> We are here in order to become, not merely to be.

The following interesting legend is about the great missionary, Saint Columban (543-615). He was poor, he only had a donkey, which walked behind him on his apostolic travels with a little luggage on its back. Once as they were passing by a thick forest, a bear rushes out of the forest and kills the donkey. What did the saint do? He turned to the bear and said: "Because you killed my donkey, now you will have

to carry my luggage." The bear, still dripping with the blood of the donkey, bent his back to receive the luggage and from then on served his new master obediently.

So never complain that you are ever so passionate, fiery, thirsty for praise, *etc.* Tame those wild bears, make them serve you. Passion itself is not a grievous misfortune, only an uncontrolled passion is. No great things get accomplished without great passions, so there are no great men and no saints without great passions.

Passion is like the wind blowing on the sea. If there is no wind, the sailboat cannot move. And if the wind starts up, there is still the question: Are we able to harness the wind to drive the sailboat?

Catholic character building does not demand the destruction of passions; instead, it wants to make them your allies. Do not ask for their advice, but use their energy; they are good helpers but bad advisors.

The will receives its firmness and manliness exactly from correctly channeled passions. Only the one "passionately" pursuing his noble goal will win despite all obstacles. The passions are wild horses before the carriage of your life; allowed to run unconstrained, they will land you in a ditch, but if firmly controlled, they will make you fly towards your goal. Every passion is like fire: it can be a blessing or a curse.

No matter what fiery temperament you have, no matter what bad dispositions you inherited (which is not your fault), do not be discouraged, do not complain. Work on ennobling your soul, and remember the great consoling truth:

Facienti quod est in se Deus non denegat gratiam–if you do everything in your power, God will not deny you His help.

As Schiller writes in *Das Lied von der Glocke:*

> Beneficial is the power of fire
> When man controls and watches it.

Getting Out of Bed on the Wrong Side

There is changing weather even in the soul. There are times of bright sunshine; at other times, you do not know why, damp fog settles over the soul. There are times when the work goes very easily, and you are in a good mood. At other times, rainy weather, unpleasantness, not feeling well ruin your mood. "He got out of bed on the wrong side," they say, and you might yourself say, "I am in a bad mood." The mood does not depend on us, so we are not responsible for it. But it does depend on us if we try to gain control of our moods, to prevent being tossed around by our moods in doing our duty. Take advantage of your good moods, work goes more easily then. But if you work only if you are in a good mood, your work will not get very far. And what will happen to him later, when he neglects his duty because he was in a bad mood? Even if you are in a bad mood, you have to force yourself to work. That is your duty, that is what you will do.

But what is the value of such work? you might ask. It will have the tremendous value of training you to fulfill your duties. It will make sure that you will dictate to your moods rather than your moods dictating to you. And remain in control of your moods not only in your work but also in your social interactions and behavior too. Even if you are in a bad mood, people will not notice a sour face, sulkiness, and grumbling. People are often ashamed of hasty words and acts that were results of bad moods. We may utter a sentence suddenly that will turn out to be hurtful or insulting to others. "I did not mean to say that! I did not expect that it will be taken this way!" Too late, it has been said.

The real worth of man comes to light in trials, dangers, and adversity. To remain hopeful even in misfortune, to stubbornly resist affliction, not to break under them, this is the virtue of the oak, of rocks, and of great souls. And the same applies to conquering bad moods.

> They have turned night into day,
> and after darkness I hope for light again.
> (Job 17:12)

In the great depths of the sea, black as night because the sunlight is not able to penetrate there, where temperature is between 2 and 4 degrees Celsius, where the water is oxygen-poor, and the weight of water creates enormous pressures (pressure increases one atmosphere for each ten meters in depth); in this forbidding environment, interestingly, the only light is generated by deep sea creatures, by what is called bioluminescence, a chemical reaction in the creature's body that creates a low-level light. Since the radiating energy of the sun cannot reach this place, the creative wisdom of God provides even for this dark place: the creatures living here generate some light.

So there is light even in the darkest depth of the sea. Therefore, if your soul is in order, do not ever be dispirited, somber, and downcast. Do not ever get out of bed on the wrong side. Be of good cheer, ready to converse with a chirping bird, and thereby conquer your bad mood. And be the source of life, joviality, light and joy when in your home the hardships of life, material cares and despondency cast their shadow over your parents.

I Have No Luck!

After receiving a bad mark, many boys cry in despair: "I just have no luck!" And when his schoolmate makes progress, he is ready to say: "Of course! That fellow is always in luck!" One is greatly mistaken to believe that success is a matter of luck, and if one expects results to be produced by luck one is waiting in vain. If one is to succeed in

life, one should not complain about lack of luck, but rather take time by the forelock and hold onto it. Don't you have a whole crew working for you? You have two strong arms, ten nimble fingers, quick feet, sharp eyes and acute ears–all ready to work for you! Moreover, you have your brain, educated and clear thinking, processing hundreds of messages arriving from your senses every minute. Why do you need outside help? Why do you need prompting from Joe in school? Or that the uncle of your grandmother will get you that cushy job? Whoever calculates that way in his youth will not be of much help to society later on.

The Muslims have an interesting saying: "The whole world belongs to God, but he rents it out to the brave." In other words, it is neither idle waiting for luck, nor searching for influential friends that befits a young man, but rather hammering out his future with hard work. Just as Horace (Quintus Horatius Flaccus, 65-8 B.C.) says it: *Multa tulit fecitque puer, sudavit at alsit*, "much from early years has he suffered and done, sweating and chilled."

You will be victorious in the struggles of life only if you are stubbornly resolved on victory, and after occasional setbacks (nobody can avoid them) get down to work again and again with renewed zeal.

> Adversity does not dishearten, success does not daze,
> Strain our forces, multiply our cares,
> Tend to the belated works of the past,
> Hoping for the best, prepared for the worst.
>   (Mór Jókai, 1825-1904)

So the most important thing is neither luck nor brilliant talent, but rather conscientious, stubborn zest for work. The sea of life is full of sad shipwrecks who lacked will power, courage, and persistence; whereas others with fewer talents but with unwavering determination are gliding towards their target.

I Tried and Failed

The reason for much dismay and despondency is confusing serious willing with mere desire. Many boys complain: "How many times I tried to give up my fault! How many times I tried to improve! All in vain, I failed." Yet, in truth, he did not mean to do it, he did not even try it, he only thought "I would like to change" but he did nothing to accomplish this goal. There is a tremendous difference between "I would like" and "I will!" The first is a tin soldier who does not scare anybody (least of all your faults), the second is a power capable of conquering the world, including your faults.

Once on a beautiful May afternoon while a student was studying, through the open window a ladybug flew in. After landing on the desk, suddenly it found itself on its back. It struggled and kicked, its legs whirring, but it could not get up. (This is "I would like.") If I remain like this on my back, I will perish, thought the bug. With great effort, it opens the wing covers on which it lies, turns on its side, (I must do so, otherwise I perish), flutters its wings, finally it is on its legs again, and victoriously takes off and soars away. (This is "I will.") The ladybug flew away, but from it you can learn the difference between "I would like" and "I will!"

"I tried and failed." I will have to tell you honestly: No, you have not tried. You have only thought it would be good to try. You are one of those who cannot get out of the cage of their passions because they are not willing to deal firmly with those passions.

"I have tried." But then why were you looking back at the forbidden fruit you were intending to leave? You know from experience how bitter the aftertaste of this fruit is, and yet you are still wishing it back! Why did you gradually compromise on your good intentions? Would Christopher Columbus (1451-1506) ever have discovered America if the first failures discouraged him? He went from country to country trying to find financial backing for his planned trip. He was ridiculed, he was called an adventurer, his plans declared impractical, yet he stuck fanatically to his goal. He had good reasons to believe he was right, and he started out on his trip, although most people were convinced they would never see him again.

Nil tam difficile, quod non solertia vincit–Nothing is so difficult but that by diligence and practice it may be overcome.

> Pull yourself together,
> You are young.
> At your age one has vigor
> And courage to succeed.
>   (Goethe)

Large parts of Zeeland, a province of the Netherlands, are below sea level. Life is a constant struggle with the sea. It has been flooded many times, yet the coat of arms of Zeeland shows a lion half-emerged from water, with the text *Luctor et Emergo*, I struggle and I emerge. Your motto should also be "I struggle and I survive."

To Wish Exceedingly

Valde velle! To wish exceedingly! These Latin words well express the road to character. Character is not the result of whining and ineffectual bursts of activity, but rather systematic, persevering self-education and making use of all our spiritual energies. When Saint Francis Xavier was canonized, Saint Francis de Sales cried out: "This is the third Francis to become a saint. I shall be the fourth!" And he kept his promise! But to accomplish that a momentary enthusiasm was not enough. Many boys "would like," "would want," say "wouldn't that be nice if it was this or that way," but otherwise do nothing else. Plan comprehensively, start with a gusto and persevere, that is the road to character. Can you imagine a more beautiful praise than the words on the tombstone of Major Dominik in Kribi (Cameroon):

> Do not look right! Do not look left!
> Forward! Straight ahead! Trust in God!
> Get it done!

It is incredible what man is capable of when he learns to will decisively and perseveringly.

There are great forces latent in us, much larger than we would think, except that they are chained. If you believe in these forces they are immediately liberated. So begin every work with the thought: This goal I shall certainly reach! If you do not believe staunchly in victory, your will is weak and eventually ineffectual. Whatever you are obligated to do, you are also able to do.

Away with the Alps!

Napoleon provides an excellent example for what incredible obstacles a firm, manly will is capable of overcoming. He was in the middle of conquering nations when he was told that the Alps were an obstacle to his army. "Then away with the Alps!" he said calmly. And thus he caused the Simplon Pass to be built. Incredible willpower! Had he not been so immensely selfish, he would not have ended in such a tragic manner. But you can learn strong will from him.

At the entrance of a medieval castle there is a single word: *Decrevi!* I have decided! An excellent motto: "I have decided, and that is the end of it. No matter what, I shall do it!" You also should see clearly your goal. And if you set that goal for yourself: death or victory!

Do you want to be a crawling worm or an eagle? Forever crawling in the dust of vacillation, writhing impotently, or soaring with your actions to the heights like an eagle? Life crowns only the heroes; the cowards receive a clown's hat. *Ad augusta per angusta:* "Through trial to triumph" or "To high places by narrow roads."

The great Hungarian poet Sándor Petőfi (1823-1849) is the author of the poem *Nemzeti Dal* (the national song). When Petőfi finished writing this poem on March 14, 1848, the first line of the original text read: "Go ahead, Magyar, the country calls!" rather than "Rise up, Magyar..." A friend of Petőfi said: "This is not good. The Hungarian first has to get on his feet before he can be told to 'go ahead.'" Petőfi immediately corrected his famous poem.

You should also rise up, get on your feet after so many comfortable "I would like" wishes, then proceed to do, will and work, instead of whining that you are too weak and that you will not succeed.

Cowardly thoughts of 　　timid procrastination, Womanly hesitation, Fearful lamentation Do not overcome misery, Do not make you free.	To persevere 　　against misfortune, Never to bend, To prove oneself strong, Will be rewarded By help of the gods. (Goethe)

Facing Fate!

It can be said of every great man: "He knew how to will!" Saint Thomas Aquinas was asked by his own sister: "What shall I do to gain eternal life?" "You have to will to gain it" was the brief answer.

It does not befit a young man to be cast down before difficulties and complications; he should rather face them bravely. Even if the sky is overcast, the sun will come out eventually. No matter how severe the winter is, spring is on its way.

The young one must never be dispirited. Work is for the young, rest is for the old. Do not be afraid! Face the difficulties boldly! Often the problems appear worse than they really are. There is an English saying: "It is not raining as hard as it looks through the window."

Read how wisely the pagan Seneca thought about this matter:

Misfortune does not break the strong man.
  (Prov. 2)

Calamity is virtue's opportunity.
  (Prov. 4, 6)

Fire tests gold; trouble tries the strong man.
  (Prov. 5, 8)

The history of great men is full of rousing examples. Many thought everything was their sworn enemy. Thousands of obstacles were in the way of their plans, but they faced them, and won.

The Calvary of Christopher Columbus lasted eighteen years in the royal courts of Europe, until finally he could start preparing his sea voyage. Do you know how old he was at this point? Fifty-eight. Others retire at that age; he was only allowed to get started at this age. Beethoven, the great composer, was deaf when writing his greatest masterpiece. Moses, the great liberator of the Israelites, had a speech impediment, but humbly accepting his fault, with the help of God, he became the great leader of Israel.

So do not be a pessimist! Do not say: "No matter what I start, it will not work out, I am pursued by misfortune." Do not say, as so many do, "If one is lucky, even his bullock will have calves, and if he is out of luck, he will always break his nose." If you think that misfortune is pursuing you, turn around and stare it down.

Do not say "the blockhead is the pet of fortune." This saying is the comfort of the lazy and the helpless, implying that he, on the other hand, is very clever. Trying to blame others, not ourselves, for our troubles is always vanity.

Listen, how the lazy boy is whining when a diligent boy receives a good mark: "Of course! Yesterday they sent a big ham to the teacher. If only we had a spare ham..." But he would never admit that he is lazy and the other one is diligent.

Listen to what a storekeeper says about another: "The man has no skin on his face. He is not averse to stealing and cheating..." But he would never admit that the other is more diligent, more skillful than he; that the other is getting ahead not with his sins but with his virtues: his zeal to work, his skills, his indefatigability, his foresight; and he himself is left behind because he is clumsy, loves his comforts, is not thrifty enough, and neglects his business.

The Famous Thirteen

Francisco Pizarro (1471-1541), Spanish conquistador, conqueror of the Inca Empire and founder of Lima, the capital of Peru, ran into difficulties in his quest, so much so that his crew demanded to return to Panama. Pizarro drew a line in the sand, saying to his men: "There lies Peru with its riches; here, Panama and its poverty. Let each man choose what best becomes a brave Castilian." Only thirteen men decided to stay with Pizarro, but these men, who later became known as the Famous Thirteen *(Los trece de la fama)* are the ones who succeeded.

So do not ever lose your head no matter what tribulation you have to face. Some men have more than their share of adversities, they are literally pursued by misfortune. If that is your portion, never mind! Never give up! Work and do not despair! You get farthest in life if you remain serene, do your duty with a smile; rejoice over your good fortune, bravely endure misfortune, and accept the advice of the Roman poet Horace:

> Remember to keep a steady mind
> in difficult circumstances.

Let us say you lost your job. A great blow. But do not despair! There is no place for you in this whole wide world?

And how do you know what God is intending for you by suddenly breaking your career? Maybe He is trying to steer you towards your true vocation, the way He did with Blessed Edmund Campion (1540-1581), a favorite of Queen Elizabeth of England. Once Campion had to display his considerable riding skills before the court of Elizabeth. He fell off his horse. Painful ridicule instead of success and applause. He came to his senses, repented, recognized his true vocation, became a Jesuit and a missionary and died as a martyr. Had he not fallen off his horse, he probably would have lost his soul.

The greatest mistake is trying to evade the trials of life by choosing death. No matter what fall, catastrophe, or shame you had to encounter in life, as long as you are alive, you can always recover and make amends. The unfortunate suicide deprives himself the only chance to make amends and adds to his sins suicide. *Palma sub onere crescit:* If we put a weight on a palm tree, it grows all the better under the weight. I do not know if this ancient belief is true, but I know that a strong man will not break under trials, but uses them as steps on his ascent.

Julius Caesar (100-44 B.C.) landed in Africa. Stepping out of the boat, he stumbled and fell to the ground. His superstitious entourage see a "bad omen" in it. Caesar keeps his presence of mind and makes the most of the situation by crying: "*Amplector te, Africa!* Africa, I embrace you!" He turned his fall into success.

The struggle and deprivation is not merely "trouble," but a source of heroic virtues. If there is no temptation, there is no self-control. If there is no trial, there is no perseverance. Whoever fights becomes stronger. Dante wrote his great work, *Divina Commedia*, in exile, in virtual poverty. Schiller wrote his most important dramas while painfully ill. Mozart finished his Requiem in painful illness.

It would not be good for a river if all the fish eggs turned into full-grown fish; it would not be good for the garden if every flower turned into a fruit; and it is not good for man to succeed in everything he starts. Lack of success teaches humility, whereas success makes one proud. Man can survive everything except continual well-being:

> Everything in the world can be endured
> Except a long series of good days.
> (Goethe)

The Danger of Success

Of course I know that success is a great motivator, and lack of success leads to discouragement. But I must warn you not to become conceited if you have had some successes. Lack of success may harm your zest for work, but imagined or too early recognition is likely to be the downfall of many more.

There are boys who, after some dabbling in painting or violin playing, are immediately declared to be a new Leonardo or Mozart by their parents and adulating friends. The boy considers himself an earth-shattering genius, an *"Übermensch,"* and starts behaving accordingly, becomes eccentric, nothing impresses him, passes condescending judgment on everything, and most importantly stops studying. "He is going to live from his talent."

I do not know if you might also be in danger of uncritical praises, having been declared a potentially world famous pianist, violinist, or painter. Whatever talents God gave you, develop them as much as you can, but do not lose your sober, balanced judgment. Do not stop your studies because you are convinced of your talents as a poet or composer. Do acquire some education or trade apart from your supposed talents to make sure you can support yourself in the future. You will find later when you grow up that all the arts are full of mediocre talents who cannot make a living with their modest abilities. And, to be honest, mankind gains more profit from a pair of well-made boots than from a volume of confused poetry.

Where Is Asia?

And if you are not supposed to overestimate the talents God gave you, what about the young men boasting of their "knowledge?" There is nothing more laughable than sixth-grade students boasting that they know everything. The teacher is "dated" and the textbook is "trash"! They know so much that they are justified to be atheists. And they might even discover gunpowder again...

I still have to laugh when I remember how a loudly boasting student, Peczkai, was unmasked. It was Latin class in sixth grade. The teacher dictated Latin sentences and we had to write down the translation in our copybook. The copybook of our "knowledgeable" friend Peczkai was full of strange translations like this:

Hannibal ante portas = Hannibal, formerly a doorman...

Caesar militibus omnibus in Galliam venit = Caesar with his soldiers went to Gallia on omnibus...

Conticuere omnes intentique ora tenebant = They all became silent, with their noses in the ink...

But there was one Hungarian sentence even the teacher could not guess how it came about. The original Latin was the well-known ode of Horace written to Mecenas:

Mecenas, atavis edite regibus! = Mecenás descending from royal ancestors!

But Peczkai's Hungarian translation read: "You eat me for dinner, but the bird eats the kings."

"Peczkai, how did you produce this, please?"

"Sir, I translated the text word by word."

"What text?"

"What you dictated: *Me cenas, at avis edit e regibus!*"

Never in my life will I forget the tremendous laughter that broke out in the class. And Peczkai stopped boasting with his knowledge. What little fraction of the immense amount of existing scientific knowledge could have been absorbed by the small student brain?

How different is the statement of Newton (1643-1727), the great scholar of nature, who described himself as picking up little shells on the shore of the ocean of truth. "I do not know what the world thinks about my work," Newton writes, "but to me it appears that my whole scientific career is like a child playing on the seashore, and although at times I may have found a more attractive stone or shell than my playmates, but on the whole the ocean of truth remained hidden from me."

It would be very good for these budding giants to consider the words of Sir Walter Scott (1771-1832), the great Scottish novelist, who said after many decades of work: "Throughout my career it was my ignorance that pained me and hindered me."

The more one knows, the more modest one becomes; and the more one studies and knows the more clearly one sees how little the wisest man knows. Not in vain said Socrates: "The ultimate of human wisdom is to know that we do not know." And Seneca writes: "Many would have become wise had they not imagined that they were already wise." And the Hungarian proverb: "If you were wise, you would not be boasting about it."

It is said about the chicken that cries a lot but gives few eggs: *Viel Geschrei, wenig Ei.*

A famous Austrian preacher and author of popular books of devotion, a Discalced Augustinian friar, Abraham a Sancta Clara (1644-1709) put it this way: "*Stultus und Stolz wachsen auf einem Holz.* Foolishness and pride have the same source."

There was a student whose younger sister, also a high school student, presumed to know everything better than her brother. After a while the brother got tired of her presumptions and said to his sister: "Edith, please do not stick your nose into these things. Listen for a minute, what language am I speaking now: v sub zero times sine of alpha times t minus g times t square per 2? It is the mathematical expression of the travel time of an object thrown at angle alpha and with starting speed v0. As you see, you do not understand a word of this." The girl became much more low key after this.

Alcibiades (450-404 B.C.) was proudly telling his master, Socrates, what large estates he owned in the vicinity of Athens. Socrates got a large map and asked: "Show me where Asia is." Alcibiades pointed it out. "Good. Now where is Greece?" Alcibiades pointed it out, it was very smaller compared to Asia. "And where in Greece is Peloponnesus?" Alcibiades could hardly find it on the map, it was so small. "And where is Attica?" It was a mere dot on the map. "And finally show me where your large estates are." Unfortunately they were not visible on the map.

So do not believe, my son, that your intellectual endowments are very large, when the greatest thinkers claim to have only a mere speck of dust. And do not imagine that you are the center of the universe, because you yourself are a mere speck of dust. And if your mate boasts too loudly ask him modestly: "Tell me, buddy, where is Asia?"

Please, Lend Me Some Money!

A great test of character is how one earns, saves, and spends his money. Try to achieve in life that you never have to borrow money. It is a difficult thing to pay it back. Even more important is it to learn that if you do not earn your own money, but others support you, you will never under such circumstances borrow money. If someone gets used to borrowing money, he is preparing his own downfall.

Douglas Jerrold (1803-1857) wrote: "Of what a hideous progeny of ill is debt the father. What lies, what meanness, what invasions on self-respect, what cares, what double dealing! How, in due season, it will carve the frank, open face into wrinkles; how like a knife it will stab the honest heart."

If you get into debt, you become, to a certain extent, a slave and thus you sold your freedom. If you cannot pay on time, you do not dare face your creditors. And if you have to, you start lying to them. You have to humiliate yourself. Rather go to sleep hungry than wake up with debts. The proverb says it well: "The empty sack cannot stand straight" and "On the back of debt rides mendacity." Anyway, there is rarely any blessing on borrowed money. Experience shows that people are more careful with money they had to work hard for than with what they just borrowed. So neither borrow nor lend money. You may have to make exceptions in certain cases, but in most cases you do well to refuse to lend money. And if he takes offense, never mind, he was not a valuable friend. True friendship should never be strained with money borrowed or lent.

An old Persian wise man was asked by a younger one: "What am I to do? So many people bother me all the time, they disturb my most valuable time." The old man answered: "To the poor, lend a small amount. From the rich, borrow a larger amount. You will never see them again." A lot of theft, cheating, embezzlement, depravity, and suicide would never have happened if the person learned to be more responsible with money in his youth.

The Devil of Money

Under normal circumstances, before the First World War, students did not have much to do with money. The parents earned the money, the parents spent the money on them, and they were given a small allowance that they had to manage. Today, by contrast, we live in extraordinary times. The madness and chasing of money, *auri sacra fames* (holy lust for gold), has taken over the souls of many students. Young students speculate, run after money, and just recently an eighth-grader committed suicide when he could not pay for his losses on the stock market. A terrible tragedy! So it is very timely to speak about money.

I would like you to have correct views about the value of money. One cannot exist without money, that is certain; but to live only for money is not a human existence that is also certain. Money-grubbing cannot be a worthy goal of human life because money is only a means of acquiring the most noble and superior goods of life. It may well be that today, alas, many genuflect before the golden calf just like the Jews did in the desert, and many men are still evaluated today by saying: "He owns a car and a thousand acres of land"; yet, for you it should count more to hear: "He is a thoroughly honest man."

A very rich man stated on his death bed: "For forty years I worked like a slave to accumulate my wealth, and then I spent the rest of my

life guarding it like a detective. And what did I get for all that? Food, shelter, and clothing."

Saint Bernard (1090-1153) is correct: "We acquire wealth with effort, guard it with care, and lose it with sorrow."

The Hungarian poet Gyula Reviczky (1855-1889) wrote:

> Believe not that power, glory, luxury
>   and magnificence make you happy;
> The sea quenches not your thirst,
>   only the clean little stream.
>   (Reviczky, *Dicsvágyónak*)

So we are not allowed to accumulate wealth by honest means? Yes, we are allowed to do so. But if someone possesses great wealth, he is then capable of doing much good to his suffering fellow men, and therefore he is guilty of sin if he fails to do so. This is a beautiful teaching of Our Lord Jesus Christ that one is allowed to accumulate great wealth in one hand only on condition that it is used for noble works of mercy. We do not have to be communists, we do not have to deny the legitimacy of private property to realize that the huge wealth that is often seen in this world could not have been accumulated by the efforts of a lone individual; that the extreme efforts of a multitude must have gone into it, and therefore it must be used for the common good.

The proverb *Noblesse oblige*, nobility obliges, is known and kept by many. But it is also true that wealth obliges–obliges one to help and to give.

Heed the serious words of Roman emperor Constantine the Great (272-337): "To become emperor is a matter of fate; but once fate places you on the throne, try to fill the role worthily." So I especially urge you, my son, that if God gave you rich parents, endeavor to acquire a Christian way of thinking about social problems.

Karl Ludwig Börne (1786-1837), a German political writer, wrote: "The heart is hardened by wealth faster than an egg is hardened by boiling water." If you are the son of an industrialist or merchant, always consider how many hundreds of miners sweated in dark underground mines, how many workers had to stand next to fiery foundries or dangerous rotating machinery, and how many were injured by accidents performing heavy labors for your father to acquire the great income. And families, wives and children, depend on these workers, children just like you except often they have barely enough to eat.

If you entertain such thoughts, you will find ways to help them according to your means; but most importantly a serious understanding will take root in you, very rare among the wealthy today, that your wealth is merely a loan from God and one day you will have to give a thorough accounting about its use. Believe me, my son, that if such thinking was common among the wealthy, although this is basic Catholic teaching, the so-called social question, which presents such a great danger to society today, could be solved in one day.

> Rejoice over the great benefits of great wealth,
> So that you can give much to your country.
> (Ferenc Kazinczy, 1759-1831)

Not only for your country, but also for your fellow men. A rich man, who started out from great poverty, was once asked how he acquired such great wealth. "My father impressed upon me two truths: never to play until I finished my work, and never to spend money I have not yet earned" was the answer. Simple words that contain great wisdom. Do not squander money that is not yet yours! As long as you are supported by someone else, you cannot be called self-sufficient, cannot be called a man. Of course that is necessarily true for students. They are supported by their parents. But you must make sure you do not spend a penny unnecessarily. And do not ever buy anything on credit, *i.e.*, do not spend money today that will be yours only tomorrow. Always spend less than your income. Many people are unsatisfied, not because they have no income, but because they cannot reduce their expectations. Rich Hungarian landowners, possessors of great wealth, became poor because they did not obey this rule and did not believe what a hero in Sir Walter Scott's novel states: "More souls were executed by dull (or blunt) money than bodies executed by sharp sword." And people on modest incomes can live well without material worries if they know how to be thrifty.

Many boys do not know how to manage money. If they pass in front of a pastry shop, a photo shop, a sports shop, a movie theater, or a shop selling stamps for stamp collectors (depending on what their weakness is) and they have some money in their pocket, they cannot control themselves. Such a one will never be content, will never have enough money, because all money will melt in his hands like snow in warm sunshine.

How Are Monkeys Caught?

Do you know how natives in India and Africa catch monkeys? In a most ingenious way! A strong leather pouch which contains rice, a favorite of monkeys, is fastened to a tree. The pouch has an opening just large enough for the monkey to stick its empty paw in, but when it grabs a handful of rice it cannot withdraw its paw. Its fist won't go through the small hole. Poor monkey goes to the tree, reaches into the pouch, and fills its paw with rice. But now it cannot withdraw its paw. Its captors appear; poor monkey screams, but in vain. It is caught. Yet all it would have to do is let go of the rice and it would be saved. But no, it is not willing to give up the rice.

Take care, my son, lest the love of money make you a captive of the passions. I repeat: It is not possible to live without money. The big question is: who serves whom. Money should serve us, rather than our becoming its slaves. The money is a mere means: take care not to see the acquisition of money as the ultimate goal. Money can be a

good servant, but woe to you if it takes over, and for the bowl of lentils of material advantages you sell the birthright of the firstborn of God, the ideal moral values of your soul.

When somebody dies, they ask: "How much wealth has he left behind?" Yet this is not the important question. They should ask: "What good deeds did he send ahead, to his judgment?"

No matter how rich you are, you will not live forever!

The human spirit was able to conquer and restrain many evil forces, it subjugated fire, steam and electricity; likewise the Christian spirit is able to put the evil of money to the service of its noble goals.

Here I should mention, although I very much hope you do not need it, how morally destructive playing for money is. Playing cards can occasionally be tolerated if it is not for money. This is a way of passing time that does not refresh; students sit a lot anyway, their recreation should involve moving about. But playing cards for money can never be approved for a serious young man. A company of card-playing men is not becoming for a young man of character. The atmosphere there, the way of talking, the strained nerves are most likely to shake the moral refinements of the participants. Not to mention the collapse of promising futures that started at card tables, continued with usurers, and ended in suicide. This is the story of many members of the Hungarian middle class and aristocracy.

And do not think that worship of money threatens only grownups. A poor boy may have a rich and wasteful classmate for whom studying is only a part-time occupation, and his main occupation is revelry; woe to him if he gets deceived by the "favors" of the rich classmate and he also starts squandering the carefully earned money of his parents. It is the height of irresponsibility for the boy to squander the money that cost so dear to his parents.

Do not live beyond your means.
It is a great danger to have more
expenses than income.

Live Within Your Means

You may not believe this: If you want to become well off, the most important thing is not how much you are able to earn, but how well you can economize. "Who is the richest?" the Stoic philosopher Kleanthes (331-232 B.C.) was once asked. "Whoever is satisfied with the least," he answered.

If we have modest demands and expectations in a material sense, that is the best way to promote our material progress and to obtain our eventual independence. The more you can reduce your needs, the more you can regain your independence. The modern world is supremely skillful to create in man new material needs by the day. But if two youths start out in life with equal talents and equal diligence, the one with fewer needs and expectations will get farther. Having few needs is in a sense a separate source of income. The more needs one has the more one is a slave of pleasure-seeking. Why so much cheating, embezzlement, and stealing? Because people insist on their pleasures and they are unwilling to renounce anything. Why so many unhappy and miserable lives? Because they spend more than what they had. Why so many suicides? Because they focused on their desires but neglected their duties.

No matter how poor you are, you should save up some for unforeseen illness, for mishaps, and for old age when you are not able to earn money any more. No matter how much you earn, if you spend it all you are teetering on the verge of poverty. You do not have the confidence and sense of security that some savings, no matter how small, provide you with. One can save even from the most modest income, whereas if you spend everything you earn you do not get ahead at all.

But thriftiness must be learned in our youth. It forms character, whereas squandering makes one irresponsible and leads to collapse and financial failure. Yet why so few thrifty boys? Because this is not an easy task.

"But I am such a poor student, how shall I get started on being thrifty?" First of all, keep track of all your income and spending. Most importantly, never spend more than your income. And never spend money on unnecessary, superfluous things. If you buy things you do not need, soon you will have to sell things that you do need. Just look at the man who is vain. How many unnecessary expenses he has merely because "others do it too" (smoking, fancy clothes, partying, sweets). The vain man spends a lot for the sake of others, so usually he does not even enjoy the results of his expenditures. How many went bankrupt merely because they wanted the same clothes, hat, theatre, horse, and car "which the other had."

Especially, I repeat, spend less as long as you spend the money of your parents and not your own. When you are spending your own hard-earned money you will be more careful about how you spend it.

I am unhappy with the Hungarian expression for earning money: we say that we "search for money" (a pénzt "keressük"). It gives the impression that it is something easy. The English "makes" money, the German "deserves" money (Geld verdienen). Hungarian people "search for money," and if they find it they will quite easily spend it too.

Frugality has another advantage: even the poorest boy gets a chance to do good once in a while. And that gives a spiritual joy that the young man should not be deprived of. It is a beautiful thing to donate the gifts of your rich parents to your poor school mates. Even more magnificent joy it is to give to the poor something that was laid aside by denying yourself. If someone can curtail his needs and is able to be thrifty, he can do good even from a modest income. Maybe even more than the rich with great demands and needs.

> Absence of desire is the greatest of riches.
> (Seneca)

The Joys of Work

Count István Széchenyi (1791-1860), one of the greatest statesmen of Hungarian history, wrote in his book Credit: "The true power of a nation comes from the number of trained and educated human minds....Not from fertile lands, not from mountains and from mines come power but from the intellect that is able to use them."

Will a comfortable and lazy boy ever make a useful member of society? Can a country be built by shallow and dissolute youth that has an aversion to work? If he works as little as he is forced to when young, will he fulfill his duties when grown up? When in fact the slothful is his own worst enemy. The life of someone who has everything is unbearably painful. Time flies when you work, whereas time hangs heavy on the hands of the idle. Wasting time is the most painful work of man.

What is the idle missing? The joy of work. Work is the most important means of shaping character: it teaches self-control, self-denial, perseverance, and attention. What a great blessing work is you learn only if you are forced to be idle for a long time, say, because of a serious illness. The sentence of prisoners can be made more serious by depriving them of the opportunity to work and they have to sit in their cells for days or for weeks without anything to do. One can go mad that way.

Roman emperor Septimius Severus (A.D. 145-211) was lying in bed severely ill in Britain in 211. A tribune entered and asked for the slogan of the day. "*Laboremus*. Let us work," answered the emperor, the sick emperor. He knew that duty is inseparable from life, and ends only when the coffin is nailed over us.

Without work, life is empty and vain daydreaming. The spirit of slothful man becomes vacillating and his will atrophies. Work, the ever-repeated small exertions really develop the strength of will. If you work, you do not have time to be dissatisfied, to be a malcontent over your life. If you are immersed in work and perform it with zest, it can even banish smaller illnesses such as a toothache or a minor increase of temperature. We simply forget them, overcome them if we work with devotion.

I wish that the idlers, the lazy students would once consider what a great privilege it is for them to be allowed to study. Other young men have to earn their living by working with their hands, with machines, with tools and plows, and therefore many interesting things will forever remain hidden for them. But you, when you study or read, see heroes rise from thousand-year-old graves, sages long dead talk to you, world famous poets tell you tales, nations long extinct come to life, the plans and thoughts of great men revive; whoever cannot study will never know about these things. While you hear about the life of the deep sea, about the greatness of distant stars, learn about the wonderful laws of nature... You should be grateful that you are allowed to study. A truly conscientious student rejoices over these, and studies as much as he possibly can. And after having spent a tiring afternoon with his books and sitting down to dinner, he feels the satisfaction and joy of work as described by Schiller in *Lied von der Glocke:*

> Sweat must be pouring from the hot brow
> For the work to do credit to the master.

I Had a Headache

Let us look at a certain type of student, usually well dressed, but with an empty soul, who is characterized by refusing to study. I get a bad feeling when I hear from this calculating student the excuse: "Sir, I was not able to prepare for today because I had a headache." Had a headache? No, he was merely lazy. I would like to show these the many talented but poor boys who would like to study, but cannot afford it. Or if they manage to get into a school, they can only stay at the price of incredible hardships.

Whereas these others always "have a headache." Laziness has eroded their will power so much that merely getting off the sofa and looking for a textbook is real physical suffering for them. They may study half an hour an afternoon but they know nothing next day in class. Schiller said it well:

> Only serious dedication which does not shy away from hard toil
> Will be rewarded by the deeply hidden source of truth.
> Only the hard blow of the chisel
> Will conquer the hardness of the marble.

Every living man uses much of the world's resources (food, clothing, *etc.*), and something must be done in return.

We should pay for resources used with work; whoever does not work is merely a burden on society, he does not help replenish what he used up. Saint Paul says it with such remarkable brevity: "if any man will not work, neither let him eat" (2 Thess. 3:10). And not only those have to work who have pressing needs. No, even if you are rich, you still have to work.

Idleness leads to moral deterioration and intellectual backwardness. If you do not study, you are not able to judge the world correctly, you become the slave of more learned ones even if you seem to have a leading position. On the other hand, if you work diligently you may become an intellectual leader of mankind whose word will be heard for centuries long after your body has turned to dust. The great classic poets still speak to us with a vivid freshness from their masterpieces. Plato still teaches wisdom, Virgil and Dante still sing, Shakespeare still shakes our souls, centuries after their deaths. The result of work is a monument more lasting than bronze–*monumentum aere perennius.* May those who always have headaches consider this.

The Bee and the Bumblebee

It is not an accident that the bee is considered the model of diligence. The perseverance with which it moves all day long from flower to flower collecting honey is truly remarkable. There is a similarity between the bee collecting from flowers and the student studying among his books. Men have to collect and accumulate the knowledge required for life from many books, experiences, and observations with untiring diligence.

But there is a further similarity between bees and students. Both have a less admirable relative. The relative of the honey bee is the bumblebee. It is quite like the honey bee, it moves around from flower to flower, but after a full day's activity it returns home without any honey. The comparable relative of the diligent student is the lazy student. He also sits in front of an open book leafing through it just like the others. He stares at the pages as if collecting knowledge from them. His mother says with sympathy: "My poor son, you are studying yourself to death" when in fact he is only pretending diligence. His mind is wandering; his thoughts have nothing to do with studying.

The Book of Proverbs in the Old Testament presents the lazy man: "The sluggard willeth and willeth not" (13:4) and "Desires kill the slothful: for his hands have refused to work at all" (21:25). His whole life is a series of fruitless desires and sighs. He can never decide to do anything on time. In every task he sees ten times the difficulty it really contains, and he tries to hide from work: "The slothful man saith: There is a lion without, I shall be slain in the midst of the streets" (22:13).

This algebra is terribly difficult, impossible to learn, he says, and closes the book before he would have started on it. He dips into every subject, he samples everything but he does not really know anything. Poor, poor lazy student, he squanders the best years of his life.

The Injured Crane

There are boys who have perfected laziness to an art, and they can waste eight years of middle school so that they would gain as little benefit from it as possible. They do attend school (they are obliged to do so), but they are only halfhearted in their presence. And the other half? They are probably thinking about the soccer game coming up that afternoon. They keep an eye on the teacher and the other eye on a mystery story under the desk top. If the teacher starts moving around, they stare at him with full attention trying to look as intelligent as possible.

I truly pity these young men. They do two half-works, but both are worthless. They do believe that they can pay attention to two things simultaneously, but psychology contradicts that. Their time goes by just as the time of those who paid full attention to the class; except those have already learned the material whereas these did not.

A flock of cranes was flying in the autumn sky. Interestingly, one sad-looking crane could not keep up with the rest.

The poor thing must have gotten into a fight and some of his feathers were pulled out, so he had to work twice as hard as the others just to avoid being completely left behind. This injured crane is much like the student discussed above: he works too but makes little progress.

Ibsen (1828-1906) in his *Peer Gynt* depicts the state of just such a man as being surrounded by the squandered gifts and valuable hours of life. They say to him: "We are the thoughts that you should have thought. We are the songs that you should have sung. We are the tears that you should have cried. We are the deeds that you should have performed."

I would like every young man to put on his desk the following serious words that can be found on the grave of a famous merchant:

Never forget that one of the main tasks
of our existence is work.
Time is money; do not waste a single one
of your minutes, but keep track of each.
Do for your fellow men what you expect from them.
What you can do today, do not postpone till tomorrow.
What you can do yourself, do not delegate to others.
Do not covet what belongs to others.

Consider the smallest trifle important.
Do not spend what is not yet yours.
You should increase rather than decrease your earnings.
Let all your actions be governed by a strict order.
Strive to do as much good in your life as possible.
Do not deprive yourself of comforts
yet live in honorable simplicity.
Therefore, work diligently till
the last minute of your life.

Whoever likes honey should not be afraid of honey bees.
The Hungarian Benedictine Gergely Czuczor (1800-1866) was correct when he wrote:

Must have happened long ago, and only once and foolishly,
That the plums fell into man's mouth.

The idiomatic expression "plums fell into man's mouth" expresses sheer luck.

Flickering Candlelight

There are peculiar young men who are busy all day long, yet because of a lack of persistence they never accomplish anything. They are always busy doing something, but they spend no more than ten minutes on anything; they group their busy idleness so that it appears as feverish activity. Let us look at his afternoon. After lunch he starts looking up Latin words. Three minutes later he is copying a drawing. Soon after that he is lying on the sofa loudly boning up on the Napoleonic wars. Suddenly he closes the book because he remembers that he has to finish developing some photographs. After reading seventeen pages from a Gardonyi novel, he proceeds to solve a physics problem. He barely copies the formula for focal length in optics, $1/f = (n-1) * (1/r1+1/r2)$, when he turns his attention to the fly walking on his copybook, catches it, and puts its wing into his microscope. And with this fortunately ends his afternoon of studying. His mother is very sympathetic: "My dear son, how much you have studied." When in fact he only pretended to study.

It is recorded about Roman emperor Domitian (A.D. 51-96) that he often locked himself into a room, and it was forbidden to disturb him as if he were immersed in the weightiest matters of state. When in fact he was merely catching flies and sticking them through needles. He was just like the student who puts *Res Romanae* in front of him seriously frowning just to switch to the sports magazine the moment his mother leaves the room. The dissipated, disorganized work not only tires one more than serious study, it is ultimately worthless. The human mind cannot concentrate on several things simultaneously. Such young men may study, but they will master nothing. They may pay attention, but they will commit nothing to memory. It is infinitely more valuable to study for three hours with undivided attention and then play and enjoy yourself for another three hours, than to sit over your books for six hours without really studying and then get up completely unsatisfied from your half-hearted effort at your desk. Your studying is most successful if while studying you forget the whole world, you forget your surroundings, you forget your cares and worries, and concentrate with all your might on the task at hand.

It is easy to see that if you try to dance the quadrille while pondering Carnot's theorem of thermodynamics you are going to fall on your face. Similarly, you are likely to fail your physics if your mind is constantly on the dancing school. So don't start all kinds of things all at the same time; do only one thing at a time, but if you started it bring it to its conclusion.

What you do, do thoroughly!

It is a current quite mistaken belief to consider men "active" and "creative" only if they start up numerous things all at the same time.

What folly! Great discoveries and inventions were always the result of painstaking perseverance at a quiet desk, in the silent laboratory or the depths of great libraries. The great accomplishments of science, literature, art, and industry never come from inconsistent haste, rather from years of concentrated effort. You cannot get to the great mountain peaks by a single heroic jump. Instead, what is required is the unceasing work of thousands of little steps, the efforts of climbing rocks, avoiding obstacles, and occasionally even the danger of slipping.

Believe me, my son, the real hero in life is not the one able to do fearlessly a few great deeds, but the one who can carry out the numberless little deeds of his life courageously. After lunch you would like to go to sleep, but you start doing your algebra: that is courage! In the morning you would much prefer to stay in your warm bed, but when the time comes you promptly get up: that is courage! When the May sunshine tempts you to go out and play, but you are not yet finished with your homework, so you force yourself to stay with your books: that is heroic courage! When you do not feel like doing something but you still do it gladly because God commands it: that is heroic courage!

The Tortoise and the Hare

The tortoise and the hare prepared for a great running race. The finish was at the edge of the forest. The tortoise started the race with great diligence, he was sweating and straining. The hare, on the other hand, was lounging in the open field in the sunshine with great confidence and said mockingly: "You fool! You are wasting your time! One or two jumps and I have passed you." The tortoise kept on crawling, sweated, worked, and then the hare realized he was almost at the finish line. The hare made a desperate effort but it was too late, the tortoise had beaten him.

Perseverance and diligence conquered talent. In intellectual work also the main requirement is perseverance. There is much truth in the French saying: the genius is nothing but patience–*le génie c'est la patience*. I could show you a long series of young men with great talents whose downfall was taking things too lightly. In high school they received the absolute best grades even though they did not have to make any special effort for them. However, out in life they accomplished nothing because they had never learned to work systematically, to work with perseverance. Their talents have been ultimately wasted.

At the same time many men successful in life had only mediocre talents, but they compensated for it by untiring industry. To be able to "learn easily" is a very dangerous gift. "I do not have to work, I have talent," many boys may say. Unfortunately, talent is not yet knowledge, only a means to acquire knowledge. And many a talented boy dropped out of high school or university because he could not convert his talent into accomplishments.

Virgil knew this already: *labor omnia vincit improbus*–hard work conquers all.

The tortoise can conquer the hare.

Genius or Diligence?

Stubborn, tenacious work, long enduring patience is like water flowing peacefully for hundreds of years: it creates a deep river bed for itself. Only a very small percentage of people are geniuses, but everybody can select for himself a lofty goal which he then follows with stubborn perseverance all his life. The skeleton, the spine on which the successful life rests is the ultimate goal never to be lost from sight. Even the man of genius has as his characteristic the devoted, passionate attachment to some branch of science or art. The greatest accomplishments of science and art, which brought the most glory to the human spirit, are not due to some momentary flare-up of genius, but rather to the unflinching perseverance of tireless industry. So the beautiful results of energy and will power are available to young men of moderate intellectual attainments also. The great secret of success in earthly life is: are we able to be stubbornly attached to some lofty goal? The difference between a great man and the average man is only in the strength of unbending will devoted to achieving the desired goal; the great man has it, the average man does not.

Perseverance, diligence, and work did incomparably more good to the world than genius or sparkling talent ever did. Hard working brings its reward.

> Seizes his sword, jumps on his horse,
> Battles, struggles, sweats day and night,
> Not resting till he is victorious.
>
> (Czuczor, *Hunyadi*)

The motto of many students is: "Hurry up! Let us get it over with." Is that really so? Do you know how long Dante worked on the *Divine Comedy*? Exactly thirty years. And Dickens says that every one of his books cost him an enormous amount of work.

William Hickling Prescott (1796-1859), the famous American historian, was almost blind when he started work on his book *The History of the Reign of Ferdinand and Isabella the Catholic*; he realized that he must know several modern languages, so he devoted ten years to studying languages.

Newton rewrote his *Chronology of Ancient Kingdoms* fifteen times until finally he was satisfied with it.

When the great painter Titian sent one of his paintings to emperor Charles V he wrote: "Your Majesty, I worked on this picture for seven years, almost every day, and often even at night."

Virgil worked on the *Aeneid* for ten years, and before his death he wanted to destroy it because he did not consider it good enough.

Fénélon (1651-1715) revised his famous work on education, *The Adventures of Telemachus,* eighteen times.

Edison (1847-1931) read a lot even when he was a young boy. He spent half the night reading books on mechanics, chemistry, and electricity.

Leo Tolstoy (1828-1910) was very critical of his own works; he usually revised his writings three times.

George Stephenson (1781-1848) worked on perfecting his locomotive for fifteen years.

James Watt (1736-1819) worked on his steam engine for three decades.

Frederick William Herschel (1738-1822) constructed four hundred telescopes requiring great patience and perseverance.

So even men of undoubted genius are helped greatly by patience and perseverance. When Newton, a great genius, was asked how he made his discoveries, he answered modestly: "By thinking about them all the time." When he wanted a rest from a certain topic, he merely switched to another one.

A good example of what great results can be produced in later age by practice and self-discipline started early is Robert Peel (1788-1850), Prime Minister of England and a great speaker of the British Parliament, who was able to contradict the arguments of his political opponents with his remarkable power of memory. As a child he was mediocre, so how did he acquire this remarkable ability to remember?

When he was a small child, when they came home from church, his father made him repeat the sermon he heard in church. First he could not do it, but eventually the long practice sharpened his mind so that he was able to repeat the sermon word by word. And this was the secret of his success in political life.

Stephenson, the inventor of the locomotive, did not go to school; his parents could not afford it. He had to work at a machine twelve hours a day, so he used some of the time of the night to learn to read and write. He was nineteen years old when he was first able to write down his name. And what joy it was for him to educate himself in his spare time! During lunch breaks he solved math problems written by chalk on the side of a coal wagon.

In the Trenches

Unfortunately, the Hungarian temperament is not very suitable for tenacious, persevering work. The Hungarian tends to become enthusiastic very easily, but it is not his strength to persevere with quiet, regulated work. As they say, he does not have *"Sitzfleisch."* In the First World War Hungarian hussars heroically charged machine gun installations (and they often perished there), but it was not to their liking to sit patiently in the trenches for weeks. But that war was dominated by trench warfare, just as life is also mastered by patience rather than by bursts of enthusiasm. This is something you will have to learn, even if getting started with it is hard.

This "active patience" created with enormous amounts of work the Egyptian pyramids; this caused the writing and copying of Greek and Latin classics by medieval monks throughout many lifetimes at flickering candlelight; this patience caused the learning by close observation of the laws of nature and put them, one after the other, into the service of men.

There is a Hungarian saying: Patience produces roses; *i.e.*, good things come to those who can wait. Patience produces not only roses, but also knowledge, learning, and culture. Our great poet Vörösmarty in his poem "Hymnus" is asking God to make the Hungarian a persevering worker:

> God help! God of nations!
> Make this nation a persevering worker
> So that whatever his giant hands
>   set out to do
> They should always finish.
> Grant that it should not expect
>   as an unearned price
> What human hands and human
>   minds can secure.

The great composer Haydn said: "The secret of art is to devote all our energies to what we set out to do."

Besser unbegonnen, als unbesonnen! It is better not to start something than to proceed heedlessly with it.

The greatest misfortune for a young man is if he is unable to carry out systematic, persevering work. The precondition of every progress is a tireless diligence, a measured but constant effort rather than random bursts of activities. The lazy student prepares for the exam with a great burst of energy. But how can that compensate for doing nothing for ten moths?

You should adopt the motto of a Polish order of knights founded by Wladyslav IV in the seventeenth century: *"Vicisti vince!"* Have you won? Great! Rejoice over it! But do not become overconfident! Continue to fight and to win!

Training of the Will

Emotions, imagination, and temperament have a strong influence over the human will. These we do not fully control, therefore our will is not completely free. You must have experienced this: one morning you wake up with sad, depressed emotions, at other times you would like to jump with joy, but you have no explanation for either one.

It is the same with your imagination. Once without any special reason your memory starts dwelling on bygone days, or alternatively impossible thoughts or illusory pictures take shape in your head. Where did they come from? Why exactly now? You could not say.

Indeed, how much trouble is caused by our imagination! It paints pictures of insurmountable difficulties about our work in front of us to discourage us from doing that work. When you go to the dentist, the most painful thing is not the procedure itself, but the waiting in the dentist's waiting room during which our imagination tortures us with pictures of the approaching pain.

We must draw the appropriate conclusions! If we are not completely in control of our emotions and imagination, we must consciously extend our control over these territories. Take control of your emotions and imagination! You woke up in a bad mood? Never mind! Force yourself to smile, sing a cheerful song, and to some extent you have already conquered your emotions. You have to solve an algebra problem? Your imagination suggests frightening pictures: this is an incredibly difficult problem, it will make you sweat! You should counter by saying: "Oh, no, my friend, my imagination! You are misleading me, it is not so terrible, it only appears terrible. The difficulties are not nearly as great as they appear. I am going to do it nevertheless!"

As you are beginning to see, training the will involves conquering our spiritual faculties that influence the will (intellect, emotion, memory and imagination). But training the will is not merely practice to strengthen it but to make sure that this strong will is perfectly in the service of accomplishing higher goals, that it is subservient to the control of the soul.

If you want to develop a strong character, you must be able to command your emotions more effectively. Many sins such as lack of love, envy, malicious enjoyment from the suffering of another, sudden insults, and many fights are caused not by a bad will but rather by a weak will that has not yet learned to control emotions that spring up suddenly. It is easy to control a small bad mood, yet many people suffer from it because they cannot be bothered to control it. So correct training of the emotions is really training of the will. The emotions influence the will not only merely to will, but to will with zest and perseverance. It is easy to see that good deeds are more likely to spring up from the warmth of the heart than from the cold light of the intellect. Another reason to take care of educating your emotions is that will, operating without emotions, can easily turn man into a cold-hearted, selfish, stubborn, and obstinate "willing machine," which would again be a mere caricature of a true young man of character.

The wise man not only tries to overcome his unpleasant emotions and substitute for them cheerful ones, but strives to preserve the peace of his soul under all circumstances. Body and soul are strongly interdependent in us. If you are depressed and sad without any reason, force a smile on your face, rub your hands together with apparent pleasure, and lo and behold, your sadness is beginning to disappear. On the other hand, if you suffer from pain, occupy yourself with pleasant thoughts, and the pain is partially forgotten. Always try to benefit from all misfortune. *Deficiendo discamus*, let us learn from our mistakes. Your wallet was stolen on the bus? Instead of stamping with rage, consider carefully how you could have been so careless, and how you will be more careful in the future. Somebody stepped on your feet? Instead of expressing anger, say to yourself: "For this pain, I shall purchase for myself some self-control."

> Would you like to be a powerful sovereign?
> Become master over yourself!

Always to remain in control of our emotions, never to be carried away by them, is a high degree of spiritual perfection. And thus we have arrived at the most important part of this book: "the means of forming character."

CHAPTER THREE

The Means of Forming Character

I will! This word has enormous power. Through it the impossible becomes possible. If you see the Alps covered with snow and glaciers, you say: "It is impossible to get across these!" By contrast, Hannibal and Napoleon said: "I will! I must! It will be done!" and they crossed the Alps with whole armies.

Before the Battle of Lissa in the Adriatic Sea in 1866, Austrian Admiral Wilhelm von Tegetthoff (1827-1871) wanted to issue from his flagship the rallying cry *"Muss der Sieg von Lissa werden! Lissa must become victory!"* No sooner had the first word *"Muss..."* been transmitted than the battle started. So the rallying cry remained the mysterious word *Muss*, which helped to carry the Austrians to victory over the Italians. I must! I will! A powerful word.

At one time, when I was teaching high school in Eger, we went for a whole day's excursion into the Bükk Mountains. The day went very well, we enjoyed ourselves, and to be truthful, misjudged the time. When we thought to look at the clock, it was 6:30 p.m. Returning to

Eger will take two hours, and the boys promised to be home by eight o'clock.

What were we to do? I called them together. "Boys, we are in trouble. It is 6:30, you promised to be home by eight, and we have a two-hour long walk in front of us. Are you determined to be home by eight?" "Yes" was the answer.

They were good boy scouts and started a forced march towards Eger. Singing many songs, marches and boy scout songs helped maintain morale. Five minutes after the church bells finished ringing eight o'clock, our group appeared in Eger covered with dust, but carrying flowers and singing songs. We had covered the distance in one-and-half hours. How was it possible? With the help of one magic word: I will! I would like it if this word became a reality for you too, my son. The will is an enormous moving power.

> I will! That word is mighty,
> If one speaks it earnestly and calmly.
> The one word "I will"
> Can bring down the stars from heaven.
>   (Father Halm)

Are you able to will? Oh, yes, you say it often: If I wanted I could do it. If I wanted I could get top grades. If I wanted I could be punctual. If I wanted I could say my morning and evening prayers.

Quid quisque possit, nisi tentando nesciat says the Latin saying. How much you are capable of doing you will know only after you tried it once. Yes, and only "if you wanted." But try it once, want it and will it!

I Could If I Wanted

The source of most of our faults is that our will is weak. If our will were strong we would get rid of most of our faults.

The tyrannical Roman emperor Caligula said once: "I wish all Romans taken together would have only one head so I could cut it off all at once." The only head you have to cut off is the weakness of your will.

Many boys keep on repeating: "I could do this or that if I wanted to." Always "if I wanted to." Supposedly he has will power but he never tried it. At the trial it may turn out that he only thought he had will power. These young men are like painted soldiers, always ready to shoot, threatening with fierce faces that "I am ready to shoot," but nobody is afraid of them because they will never shoot.

There is no art in the world so refined as cultivating our own soul, because there is no material, marble or fine metal, in the hands of any artist to be shaped and formed that is as valuable as our soul is.

You have heard that man has free will; I am afraid you may have heard it all too often. Man truly has free will, but his will is not strong. Yours is not strong either, until you make it strong. Nobody is born with a strong will; it is a precious gift that we each have to gain by a serious struggle. You cannot grant yourself strong will effortlessly; you cannot declare: "From now on I have strong will." On the contrary, you have to work for it very hard.

The will of every boy is strong to the degree that he worked to acquire this precious treasure, to the degree that he liberated himself from the oppression of the senses. What else is spiritual freedom but self-discipline, the rule of noble sentiments over the senses and the material desires of the body? The will in your soul is like the seed sown; if you carefully nurture it, it grows up to be a great oak tree capable of resisting a storm; but if you neglect it, even the ants of small errors will make it disintegrate. Moral freedom is the reward for persevering, unflagging small efforts, for slow work, and for continuous self-improvement.

Among us come and go thousands of souls in chains of sin, exactly because they refuse to make the serious work of everyday efforts. "I could if I wanted!" Well then, want it! Try it! If you seriously want to become a man, then you should know how to want and will seriously.

Lack of will power and true willing differ as much as little pet dogs of old ladies differ from serious watch dogs. The little pet dogs cannot bite, cannot bark, cannot do anything useful except eat and whimper and cost a lot of money. By contrast, the real watch dog does not whimper but has a powerful bark, and when necessary will bite the uninvited intruder. Similarly, the boy with will power does not whimper but barks against the temptations of laziness and sin, and even bites seriously to chase them away.

How does this work? Just like the forced march after the excursion described above. For example, do you want to get top grades in school? "I do want them!" Then give the command: "Get the lesson for tomorrow into your hands (immediately, and not next week), and left-right, left-right start the forced march." Your desk is the anvil on which you forge your future. Do you want to be correct about your prayers? "I do want to be!" Then say your evening prayers tonight. "But I have so much studying to do." Find five minutes right now. "And in the morning I have to hurry to school not to be late." Well then, wake up five minutes earlier.

The Willful Youth

The willful youth! Today's usage gives a different meaning to this word, meaning a self-willed, stubborn, disobedient young man. I go back to the original meaning of the word. "Willful" means someone with a strong will. Spite, defiance, being headstrong and stubborn is not strong will, but a spasm or cramp of the will. Whoever is able to command his laughing muscle, his eye, stomach and ear, he is, in the good sense of the word, a willful youth.

So let us take a closer look at what a curse the lack of will power is, and what a blessing strong will power is.

(a) If someone does not have a well-schooled, obedient will, he is unable to perform any serious task. You yourself must know students who are not idle, yet they make no progress in their studies. Earlier in this book, I compared them to the bumblebee. These also work, the poor things, even more than many others, yet without any results. They are not able to focus on their studies because their will is weak. There is always a book in front of them, but it is a different book in every half an hour ("the previous one is so very boring"). They are constantly in motion, but they are afraid of any effort, without which there is no success in work. They are able to make their doing nothing appear as feverish activity. And at the end they complain with bitterness that the report card is bad despite all their work. And when they grow up? What will become of them? A man pushed by the impressions of the moment, a man without principles, a man who easily forgets his duties, a man dragging on a wretched life without plans and goals. What is the matter with them? Their will is weak.

(b) Let us look at another type. If someone does not have a disciplined will, he cannot observe anything properly. Yet correct and fast observation is an unavoidable part of learning. To be able to use your senses effectively, to be able to discriminate between important and unimportant, to be able to clearly grasp the given situation and act on it, all this requires a strongly disciplined will. But the obedient will helps you not only with seeing, hearing, speaking, and doing, but also with the opposite: when moral laws prohibit things to the senses, the obedient will helps not to see, not to hear, not to speak, and not to do.

(c) I go even further. If someone does not have a disciplined will, he cannot think properly and therefore cannot be educated properly. Recognizing the truth and acquiring it is serious work. The fickle young man is impatient in his reading too. He leafs through the book restlessly, nervously rushing through it to get to the end the sooner. He benefits nothing by it. By contrast, the one with a well schooled will reads slowly, thinking about what he reads, weighing the more important sentences. He does not accept every assertion blindly, he considers if what the author says is really true, takes notes for himself, *etc.* That is the only way to acquire new knowledge. But all that requires will power.

(d) You also need strong will to remember things. Many young men think it is a good excuse to say to the teacher: "Sir, I know the answer except I cannot remember it." If he is entrusted to do something and he "forgets" to do it, he thinks that "forgetting" is an excuse. In fact, absent-mindedness is the result of an undisciplined will (unless a neurotic disorder prevails). If you cannot remember a word, a name, or an event, do not look it up immediately (as the student with a weak will does), but make an effort, strain and sweat thereby strengthening your will. And if you have to accomplish something at a specified time, do not tie a knot on your handkerchief to remember it, but recall your task several times a day, be determined to keep on recalling it, and you will see that you will not forget it. If you keep on practicing this, you will be cured of absent-mindedness. You may gain such control of you memory that you do not even lose it during your sleep, and after long practice you are able to wake up exactly at the time you have determined before going to sleep. On the other hand, if you do not struggle against your absent-mindedness and grow up with it, you will have many difficulties in your life; if you become a railway track watchman, you will forget to set the switch correctly and cause a train to be derailed; if you become a teacher you will forget to go to your own class; if you become a lawyer you will forget to attend the court hearing; or you may even forget to attend your own wedding.

Demosthenes

Demosthenes (384-322 B.C.) lost his father at age seven, and his guardian robbed him of his whole inheritance.

Once he attended a court hearing, and having heard the excellent speech of the defense attorney, and the victory of this attorney loudly celebrated by the people, he conceived a plan to become a public speaker.

From then on he had a single goal before him day and night. But achieving it was not going to be easy. His first speech was received with so much hostility and derision that he had to prematurely terminate it. Depressed, he wandered around town all day long, until finally an old man gave him some encouragement to continue educating himself. He started again with even greater determination. He was ridiculed, but he ignored it. For months at a time Demosthenes went into seclusion and he made speeches in an underground room he constructed himself. He had a speech impediment–an inarticulate and stammering pronunciation. To correct it, he also used to talk with pebbles in his mouth. His lungs were weak, so to strengthen his voice, he spoke on the seashore over the roar of the waves and recited verses while running. Whenever he heard a debate, he went to his room, reconsidered the position of both sides and tried to decide which side was right. With this tireless, unflagging self-education he slowly shed his failings and became an irresistible orator whose speeches must be studied even today, 2400 years later, by anybody who wants to become a truly successful orator. When, as a child, he was merely a stammering little boy! What wonderful forces are dormant in man!

What a man is capable of may only come to light in moments of the greatest suffering. During the first months of the First World War I served on the Serbian front. One day our patrol found a Hungarian hussar in a swamp. The Serbs had captured him with his group, lined them up and executed them by firing squad. He survived and succeeded in hiding in the swamp, only his nose above water to breathe. After several days, when the Serbs left the area our soldiers found him and brought him back extremely weak. It was the seventh day that his only food was the grass of the swamp. I just realized what man is capable of!

You may have heard about dying people kept alive by a strong will for hours or days because they wanted to see just once more their child or wife coming from a distance to visit them. A strong will may have a healing effect on a sick body, so do not be dejected if Divine Providence gave you a weak body. Just recently have we heard about the death of Hungarian Count Géza Zichy (1849-1924), who lost his right arm in a hunting accident at the age of fourteen, yet he trained himself to become a great pianist. He was a pupil and friend of Franz Liszt, everywhere acknowledged as a great virtuoso. Imagine how crushed most people would have been losing their right arm. And yet what a demonstration of strong will in a crippled body!

You would be so much more grateful to God for your least talent, if you consider that even the greatest of men had to struggle with so many difficulties, little faults, and even illnesses.

Wallenstein (1583-1634), the great military commander, suffered from neurosis: he found it unbearable to listen to a rooster crowing.

Cardinal Richelieu (1585-1642), the famous French statesman, was terrified of squirrels.

Pierre Bayle (1647-1706), a French Protestant philosopher, could not bear the sound of dripping water.

Erasmus of Rotterdam (1466 -1536) broke out in fever from the smell of fish.

Scaliger (1540-1609), a French Protestant scholar, started trembling in his whole body when he saw milk.

Goethe (1749-1832), the great German writer, had excruciating sufferings from tobacco smoke.

Many great men in history had to live in weak, sickly bodies.

Helmholtz (1821-1894), the great German physicist, is known to have suffered from hydrocephalus.

Spinoza (1632-1677) the philosopher died early of a lung illness, perhaps silicosis, because he was a lens grinder.

Schiller (1759-1805), the German poet, philosopher, and playwright, died of tuberculosis.

Descartes (1596-1650), Kant (1724-1804), and Milton (1608-1674) each had a frail body, yet their work earned them great fame. What human will is capable of!

The soul is capable of conquering the weakness of the body. Many sickly boys look on their healthy fellows with grief and a measure of envy. Do not be sad! You cannot help that your body is weak. But even in a weak body you can learn skills, resourcefulness, and vitality.

The Great Physical Training

The cardinal rule of training the will is: Every day exercise yourself in conquests of the self however small, and after doing this for many years your will becomes strong. You need very many small practices; a single heroic decision will not give you strong will. If somebody wants to become good at gymnastics, say horizontal bar or parallel bars, for years he has to practice the most elementary motions with the arms and legs. If someone wants to learn to play the piano, for years he has to learn fingering and play the most boring scales for hours a day. Beethoven can only be played after lengthy preparations. Similarly, you cannot develop a strong will without patient, small exercises of the will. Conquering our nature tending towards evil is more challenging than exercises on the horizontal bar or any piano lesson. How do you expect to win a chess game if you do not know what the way of moving of each chess piece is? And how do you expect to display strong will in decisive battles when you cannot control yourself in small things?

Nobody is exempt from the training of the will that is required. The weaker your will, the more you need it. Everybody has germs of good and bad properties in him, and everybody is responsible whether he allows the good or the bad to gain control. A wagon does not care which way the horses are drawing it; but it goes more easily on much traveled roads. So do not complain that you have a difficult nature, because nature can be controlled and trained.

For example, you may say that yes you are ill-tempered but that you cannot help it. Your fellow sticks his tongue out at you, or a pile of books slips out from under your arm and you are already engulfed in fury. "I am sorry but I cannot help it," you say. Indeed, part of it you cannot help. That your face turns red, you indeed cannot help. That your heart starts beating faster, again you cannot help. But look. You have a clenched fist already, right? You can slowly open your hand, that you can help. Your face is already distorted, right? You can help it that you will start smiling (yes, while you are still furious!). And on your lips the not-so-polite words are already crowding? You can help it that you bite your lips and say nothing (yes, now, while you are still angry!). Try it! If you are looking in the dictionary for Latin or German words and you cannot find them easily, can you remain calm and continue searching? If you cannot understand a sentence immediately, do not start throwing the book but read the sentence again, maybe even the third or fourth time? To be angry you have to have a clenched fist, a distorted face and angry speech; if you take all these away (which you can do) your nature on the verge of flaring up, not finding the usual fuel, will quiet down and becomes more peaceful. You cannot change your nature but you can put the brakes on.

> Start eagerly, and already you accomplished much;
> Whoever started is making progress already,
> While indolent force merely rolls in the mud.
> Have you seen the flow of the mighty Danube:
> Started from a small spring, it lifts boats at the end.
> (Vörösmarty)

A snowflake has barely any weight, it looks so innocent when falling; but a lot of them sticking together can form an avalanche capable of destroying trees and houses.

The Indian Youth in the Wild

It is childish to be impressed by a face getting red in response to every word, by the clenched fist, the blustering out threats and fighting. The lack of patience and quarrels are always signs of a weak will.

Yet, why is such behavior so common? Because it is easy, it takes no effort. In impatient squabbles everything happens by itself, like a wagon rolling down hill. By contrast, self-control requires an effort: climbing from the swamp of passions up towards the mountain of victorious will. Real self-control is not the patience of a packhorse, it is not effeminate cowardliness, but strength, courage and endurance. Have you suffered a sad disappointment? Are you bored? Are you angry? Are you discouraged? Make sure that nobody can detect it in your words and behavior. That is self-control. Somebody has been annoying you for a quarter of an hour and you would really like to punch him in the face, but instead you merely touch his arm gently and say: "Be careful, I could handle you." That is self-control.

Impatience is the sign of weak will. The instincts manifesting themselves in impatience are present in animals also; but it is more fitting that man should put them under the control of deliberation and decision, *i.e.*, under the control of intellect and will. The smaller the child, the more impatient he is; he is obstinate, fumes with rage, screams; of course he cannot yet use his intellect and will, only the animal instincts work in him. But it is quite revolting when a grown-up does the same, thereby giving testimony that he is a slave of his instincts.

I am sure, my son, that you do not want to be the slave of your instincts. So observe yourself frequently: what is most likely to make you lose your temper, what can get you excited, and then start the fight against overhastiness and hotheadedness. This way you uproot a lot of unfair judgment, hasty words, and rash deeds.

It was the custom of some tribes of American Indians that when a boy reached the end of puberty and was to be solemnly initiated into manhood, prior to the initiation he was sent out into the wilderness for two weeks. He was given a bow and arrows and the strict

command: he must not kill, he must not even touch any animal. All the animals, deer and rabbits are running in his sight. The hands of the boy are trembling with excitement. All in vain, he is forbidden to shoot! What is he to do in the wilderness for two weeks? He can eat roots and berries or fast. If he can keep the rules, he will be initiated into manhood. You see, these Indians understand much better than we soft Europeans that self-control is the best preparation for the struggles of life, and the best indication of manhood.

But it is not enough to read about self-control and know about it a lot; you have to put it into practice. Knowledge is the theory of action, but action is practical knowledge. The will must be strengthened in a young age, it must be improved just like the rose is improved by grafting it when it is young. It is too late to do when it is old.

What a sad sight is a weak-willed young man! It takes him an enormous effort to make a decision, to utter a "yes" or a "no." Even worse is to start doing what he finally decided to do. Principles, independent thinking he has none, not in his last years of high school, not even when he grows up. He always watches what the others do and he does likewise. He is marionette without a will, a baby in long pants:

> A dandy, elegantly dressed,
> but of questionable character.

I Have No Will!

Who has the wretched misfortune that his will becomes so stunted? In the young man for whom everything has been made easy, whose every wish is always satisfied, who never has to deny himself, who never receives commands that he has to obey. Such as this develops a distorted will, a jellylike, spineless, aborted will.

You might say that even such boys explode once in a while. How they can brag! They are like tyrants over their parents! True, indeed, but these are not manifestations of human will but the outbursts of the unsatisfied instincts of a wild animal. The question of will power is a complex, mysterious question. Let us look at some examples.

There was a second-grade boy whose main problem was eating sweets. Nothing could be left out, he immediately ate them. At home he was scolded all the time, he was ashamed of himself, a hundred times he promised to change, but all in vain, at the first opportunity there was jam on his lips again. He said to his mother: "In vain do I promise, mother, I have no will power." Yet, quite miraculously, this same boy was an excellent sportsman, he trained for hours a day in several sports: he was good at running, jumping, shot put and also soccer. All this required lots of self-denial and lots of effort. So he could will if he wanted!

Another boy was unbelievably lazy. He was always sleepy, showing no interest in anything, always sluggish. Study he did not like, play he was not used to, and physical education he simply abhorred. He just sat, sat at his desk. Yet, he also had a will! In one direction only: all his efforts were concentrated on preventing any disturbance to his laziness. His mother scolded him, his father punished him, his fellows ridiculed him–never mind! No change to his laziness. He was straining not to give up his comforts. He also had will, for laziness.

From these examples, it becomes clear that the will of everybody cannot be trained in the same way. Youths can be classified in three ways. (1) There are fiery, lively, sprightly boys, who cannot think quietly and cannot act calmly in a composed manner; for these, restraint, self-denial and renouncing things is the most important schooling of the will. (2) Others are cheerful, they quickly start up all kinds of things but they they have no patience and endurance to finish them; they will have to be trained in devotion to work already started, in patience and in perseverance. (3) Yet others are dreamy, overly quiet; for these acting, doing things is the school of the will.

These three ways of training the will can be summarized by three words: *Abstine! Sustine! Aggredere!*

> Know how to deny yourself!
> Know how to persevere!
> Know how to act!

Abstine! (Know How to Deny Yourself!)

During the long years I spent educating boys I have suffered many bitter disappointments. I had many students in the lower grades of high school whose fiery eyes and lively intellect promised a rich harvest for their manhood, yet those hopes were destroyed in the higher grades by the cunning enemies of youth: passions, carelessness, inexperience, and temptations.

Often I am shocked to see how, following the work of these four enemies, the plant of noble idealism that is present in most boys in the lower grades withers away. But the worst of the four enemies is the first one: that softness and enervation with which the boys of today run after their passions, after the instincts of their animal nature, without offering the least resistance. Today, everybody wants "to live," "to enjoy" and "to have fun." That is why I list as the first method of the training of the will self-denial and renouncement. Constraining our senses, controlling ourselves, renouncement, restricting our desires is not an end in itself, it is merely a means of liberating the soul.

So when I emphatically recommend, my son, that you deny yourself many times in little things (*e.g.*, do your duties gladly, even if you would prefer not to, forego some entertainment, enjoyment or food even if you would very much like to have it) I have very serious reasons for doing so. Renouncement has a very noble goal: it gives wings to the soul, it gives the soul control over the body.

I know it myself that these are only schools of a strong will, but they are schools from which a strong moral life springs. There is deep wisdom in the Romans using the word "*virtus*" for both virtue and force; in Hungarian they also have the same root (virtue = *erény*; force = *erő*), meaning that there is no virtue without exerting ourselves and conquering ourselves. Both theory and practice day by day confirm and corroborate the words of Eternal Wisdom, of Our Lord Jesus Christ: "If any man will come after me, let him deny himself and take up his cross and follow me" (Matt. 16:24).

Clumsy is the gardener who does not cut the rose back ruthlessly. Just as there will be no rose on the stem that was spared by the clipper, there will be no strong will for the young man who never denied himself of anything.

What moves a windup clock? The energy stored up in the wound up spring. Well, self-denial is the equivalent of the winding of the spring. So do not think that complete self-control and constraining your desires, what I am expecting from you, is an obstacle to a strong, complete and beautiful life. On the contrary! That will save you from the withering away of your will and thousands of spiritual ills.

> The man who conquers himself
> Can be delivered from the yoke
> under which mankind labors.
>   (Goethe)

Inner freedom is obtained by self-control, and self-control is acquired by self-denial. Thomas à Kempis (1380-1471) writes from experience in the *Imitation of Christ:* The more violence you do to yourself, the more progress you will make.

The Hermit's Bunch of Grapes

Macarius (300-391) was an Egyptian monk and hermit who lived in the desert. One day there was a knock on the door of his cell, a peasant at the door saying: "Father, I bring you a beautiful bunch of grapes. Accept it, and refresh yourself by it." Macarius accepted it with thanks and blessed the peasant in return; but when he looked at the bunch of grapes he thought: "The venerable old hermit living next to me is much more in need of this." So he took it over to his neighbor. This gratefully accepted it and started thinking: "How good this would be for Brother Lazarus who is sick," and immediately he was on his way to Nazarius. But Nazarius did not even want to hear about eating the grapes: "How could I eat this? My Redeemer had to drink bitter gall on the Cross! I want to follow him." So the bunch of grapes wandered around from one cell to another, until finally it got back to Macarius in the evening. He cried tears of joy: how wonderful the brothers living around him were!

You see, my son, this was will power. These monks knew how to deny themselves. Some day try if you can to do something similar.

"No day without writing a line" was the motto of many learned men in the past. You may modify it to "No day without self-denial." Every day conquer yourself, renounce something, do something that you do not like doing.

József Eötvös was right: "We possess something only if we could renounce it if we wanted to. If we consider something indispensable, we are not its master; rather we are its slave... If somebody wants to teach people or rule over them, he should first learn to conquer himself and be a master of his own passions... The Catholic religion, when it demands self-denial from us, teaches us the same principle that is the basis of the philosophy of life."

Diem Perdidi! (I Have Lost a Day!)

Roman Emperor Titus (39-81) determined that every day he would perform a good deed. And when in the evening, examining himself, he found that he did not accomplish anything good that day he reproved himself by saying: *Diem perdidi*, This day is lost.

You also should exercise your will every day. But not in a haphazard fashion, once in a while, when it happens to come to your mind; but methodically, every day, hour by hour practice conquering yourself. You will not have to search for opportunities too hard; thousands offer themselves every day in the life of a student. Let us look at some examples.

When you cannot avoid some trouble, pain, or trial, do not snarl but endure it patiently. "I am so thirsty!" "I have such a headache!" "This shoe is too tight!"–do not complain, groan and whimper, but try to relieve your pain, and if you do not succeed, look on your crucified Lord, and endure it silently. What you have decided to do, go through with it. By hook or by crook, do it. Once you started it, never abandon it half finished. Faithfully fulfill your daily duties. Even the smallest one of them. If it is worth doing, it is worth doing well. There is your early morning battle with your pillow (which many boys lose); when the time arrives, get out of bed immediately. Control not only your bad moods but also the good ones. Be moderate even in your enthusiasm. Also in your speech and in your silence.

A good means of training the will is restraining our senses. Your eyes should not be roving. Do not look at everything that arouses your curiosity. There is a big crowd on the street and you are dying to know what is going on there. Never mind! Conquer yourself and just not go there. And control your tongue. This is incredibly difficult. Not to betray a secret entrusted to you. Not to talk about the faults of others and gloat over them. Not to gossip. Not to ridicule and mock those present, not to slander those absent. Not to be intoxicated by your own voice so that nobody else present gets a chance to speak. Not to be able to keep your mouth shut. Not to brag about your own accomplishments. And at all times stick to the truth even if it is to your disadvantage. And never lie, not even in the smallest things, even though they would lead to great advantages.

And the dining table is also a great place to practice self-denial. Do not be choosy as to what you eat, do not look for and give preference to delicacies, and do not be greedy and stuff yourself full. Many people lose control over their will at the dining table.

So, as you can see, there are very many opportunities for training the will. The training is by practice, not by reading about them. You will never learn to swim merely by reading about the strokes, you have to try them and do them. And you will never learn swinging on the parallel bar, no matter how well it is explained to you, unless you practice it every day.

Saint Paul points out a fundamental truth when he writes: "I say then, walk in the spirit, and you shall not fulfill the lusts of the flesh. For the flesh lusteth against the spirit: and the spirit against the flesh; for these are contrary one to another" (Gal. 5:16-17).

And at another place: "For I am delighted with the law of God, according to the inward man: But I see another law in my members, fighting against the law of my mind, and captivating me in the law of sin, that is in my members" (Rom. 7:22-23).

Which of you never felt in himself this tragic division, this sad two-faced nature, the struggle between good and evil, and the truth of the old saying: *Video meliora proboque deteriora sequor*–I see the better way and approve it, but I follow the worse way.

So if you desire a free, manly soul, do not recoil from the relentless struggle against your softness and love of comfort. Every day do something good, and every day deny yourself in something.

You must have heard about the heroism of King David of the Old Testament. You know that when he was young he tended the flock of his father. A bear or lion killed some of the sheep, so David pursued it and killed it (1 Kings 17:34-36). He was a heroic boy, said a second grader. David with his sling shot killed Goliath (1 Kings 17:49). This was a heroic deed, said a fourth grader. And when he fought the Philistines he was victorious over them (1 Kings 17:52). He was a hero, said a fifth grader.

Yet these are not the most impressive things about King David. Do you know what I find most impressive about him?

When the army of King David faced the Philistines between Jerusalem and Bethlehem and in the great heat every creek and spring dried out, "David longed, and said: Oh that some man would get me a drink of the water out of the cistern, that is in Bethlehem, by the gate. And the three valiant men broke through the camp of the Philistines, and drew water out of the cistern of Bethlehem, that was by the gate, and brought it to David: but he would not drink, but offered it to the Lord, Saying: The Lord be merciful to me, that I may not do this: shall

I drink the blood of these men that went, and the peril of their lives? Therefore he would not drink" (2 Kings 23:14-17).

This is what impresses me the most. What did David sacrifice? A little water. What did he lose thereby? A momentary pleasure. And what did he gain? The admiration of his soldiers, the strengthening of his will, and the grace of God since he made the sacrifice to the Lord. You see, with a swig of water you can perform a heroic deed. Even present a sacrifice to the Lord.

The Pythagoreans of ancient Greece loaded their tables with the finest of foods, famished they sat down in front of them, looked at them for a long time, then departed without ever having touched any of the food. A second grader would say: "Oh how silly they were!" But if you consider it more seriously, you are going to acknowledge the heroism of their act. These pagans understood the importance of conquering of self, self-denial and the training of the will.

You, my son, just carry out your practices of self-denial, and you will see that there are wonderful sources of joy that remain unnoticed in many souls, and cannot be made accessible and open in any other way but by the tool of self-denial. These are the deep, enduring, sacred joys that spring up in your soul whenever you gained control over an inclination or desire of yours, whenever you were able to make a sacrifice just to fulfill your duty, whenever you proved generous towards others, *etc.*

The Rooster of the Japanese Painter

According to a Japanese legend a rich merchant once placed an interesting order with a painter. The painting had to display a rooster, but that in the most perfect manner. Having placed the order, the merchant waited for many years in vain. Finally, tired of waiting he went to visit the painter to find out how the picture was progressing. There was no sign of the painting. However, the painter asked the merchant to take a seat, started painting and in a quarter of an hour he produced the picture of the rooster. Impeccable masterpiece! The merchant was elated. However, when it came to paying, the merchant was extremely surprised at the enormous amount of money that the painter asked for this work of fifteen minutes and loudly protested. The painter calmly pointed to a huge pile of drawings each depicting a rooster and said: "For three years I have been painting roosters to gain the facility to paint a perfect rooster. I now expect to be paid for this long practice." The merchant paid willingly.

Similar is the case of the training of our will. If it is our desire that our will be always obedient and perfectly carry out the good planned out by our intellect, then we need constant practice lasting decades. With the same patience the painter uses to put on the canvas the picture that already exists in his soul, we have to work on the shaping of our character.

But we will not be overwhelmed by this task. The painter also found that the next picture was easier then the previous one, and the last one took only a quarter of an hour to produce. Beginning is the hardest even in the realm of self-education. The longer you practice the good, the easier it gets. I remember when I was a student how difficult I found exercises on the still rings. I did not have the strength for the crosses. For many months I struggled building up my strength. Eventually I learned them and got quite good at them.

Similar is the case with the spiritual life: the first time it is very hard, it costs you a great deal of struggle, but the tenth time it is already quite easy. So practice every day, and then you will have a strong will. Learn to renounce things that are permitted. In the morning, jump out of bed saying: "A little self-conquest!" If your tooth is aching, grit your teeth, do not complain but say to yourself: "A little self-conquest!" You are reading a very interesting book. Close it at the most interesting part: "A little self-conquest!" You are hungry like a wolf. Do not touch your food for a few minutes: "A little self-conquest!" You can practice on thousands and thousands of similar small things. And the more you remain the master in little things, the more easily you will become the master in important things.

Let us look at an example in detail. Your parents left home, and you promised to guard the house in their absence, and you also have a lot of homework to do. Five minutes later Johnny shows up at the door: "Come on, Frank, here are the boys, let us go and play ball!" It is a beautiful sunny afternoon outside, and inside you are facing a complex algebra problem. Now the struggle starts: shall I say yes or no? I promised to stay home and guard the house. But the boys will mock me that I have spoiled their game. It would be so good to go and play, but my parents will scold me. What if I come back early and they will never know? But then what happens to the algebra problem? Tomorrow in class I could say that I was absent-minded and left my notes at home. But doing so is not honest... So the arguments swirl pro and con. The boys are getting impatient. Finally you say bravely: "Forgive me, but today playing for me is impossible..." The boys depart, and you are looking after them sadly. But you feel the satisfaction of having done your duty honorably. And if you have to do this again, the same decision will be easier the second or the third time, and eventually it will be the most natural thing for you to do the right thing without hesitation. Painting the later roosters came quite easy to the Japanese painter also.

You will have to strive for acquiring an ever-present ability to practice the good that never hesitates nor ever needs to deliberate. When you do not any more have to weigh which road to choose before acting, but you will choose the good routinely as a habit acquired by long practice, and you will shun evil swiftly and spontaneously, then life is paying you back for your long preparations. Life is not paying you with money; it is paying you with the facility with which you are able to act, easily and gladly, corresponding to your noble principles, that is to say you are now a "young man of character."

Sustine! (Know How to Persevere!)

Another method of training the will is by steadfastness, persistence and endurance. The well-known American psychologist William James (1842-1910) recommended to youths that they do something every day that they do not relish doing exactly so that they remain firm with themselves. In a German boarding school, when the students heard of the recommendation of James, they went out into the garden and chewed up live June Beetles, because that they truly "did not relish." Ugh! Childish exaggeration, yet still an impressive generosity to acquire strong will.

No need to follow this German example, no need to burn your arm in a fire like Gaius Mucius Scaevola did. The everyday life of a student is full of opportunities to practice heroic patience. Endure suffering and pain. Study patiently, never get excited or angry. Speak patiently at home, never talk back, never make faces, never be bad-tempered. If something gets you excited, annoyed or irritated, do not be indignant, but wait patiently and reason with yourself to calm down. Don't ever do anything that you would have to regret five minutes later. (This is a very important rule for impetuous young men!) And I do not only mean passive patience, endurance without words, but even more active patience, sticking to something in adversity.

Our Lord Jesus has a serious warning: "But he that shall persevere unto the end, he shall be saved" (Matt. 10:22). This is true not only about eternal life, but also about success in this life. Because of the lack of perseverance a lot of efforts might be brought to naught.

George Chavez, the young Peruvian aviator, on September 23, 1910, accomplished the feat of crossing the barrier of the Alps between Switzerland and Italy, over the Simplon Pass, in an airplane. We have to say he almost accomplished this because at the end he crashed and died from his injuries. He would have needed only just a few more minutes of perseverance; he could already see the crowd of people waiting to greet him. But his descent was too sudden, the Blériot lost a wing and crashed.

It is wise to prepare for more than what actually awaits you. If you have to have a hike of three hours, prepare for four hours. If you have to study two hours, prepare for two and half hours of studying–this way you will still have some reserves left. Stick it out! Persevere!

The following anecdote is about the Lomnice (or Lomnicky) Peak, which is one of the highest and most visited mountain peaks in the High Tatras mountains, which today belongs to Slovakia. A beautiful June morning two Hungarian students started out to climb it. Both of them were from the Great Plains region of Hungary, so they knew little about mountain climbing, and they had never seen such magnificent mountains before. They were in high spirits, walked briskly, sang merrily, and with big smiles they passed an old man who also appeared to be heading for the same peak, but moved so slowly and calmly that one of the students opined "even a snail moves faster." When they looked back ten minutes later, the old man looked like a tiny ant deep below them.

But the boys started breathing more and more heavily; first they stopped for five minutes every half an hour, later every fifteen minutes they had to lie down "for a short half an hour." By noon they were completely exhausted, and they took a long rest next to a small waterfall, when suddenly the old snail-man appears and with the same slow and calm steps passes them, and just goes, and goes, and again looks like a tiny ant except this time he is above them. And the two young students are stretched out on the rock completely helpless and exhausted. Because to reach the heights, to achieve some lofty goal it is not enough to have a youthful dash and ephemeral enthusiasm; one needs a calm and steadfast perseverance.

To Suffer without Complaint

Life is a mixture of joys and sorrows, and in many lives the sorrows dominate. *Leben ist leiden,* to live means to suffer. The life of the young man will also contain difficulties, hard trials, lack of success, failure, misunderstanding, bodily suffering, illness; and the indication of true character is how one is able to endure these trials. Endure! *Sustine!*

Many poor men, and also many poor students, often envy their richer fellows. They do not want to believe that most people have their fair share of sufferings. There are the ones who shake their fists and fulminate against fate by uttering profanities–these souls are coarse. There are the ones who whine over what they cannot change with impotent resignation, with heads bowed, with their spirits broken–these souls are weak. And finally there are those who hurt just as much as anybody else from some adversity, they hurt to be neglected, they genuinely mourn their deceased mother, they suffer from an illness, *etc.,* except that they also know that the steel of pure character is tempered in the fire of suffering endured in a resolute manner.

One can be poor and happy, or rich and unhappy. One can be sickly and happy, one can be healthy and unhappy. One can be blind and happy, or unhappy with two healthy eyes. It all depends in what spirit we accept suffering. I want to use suffering for the perfection of my character! I know that pain endured in the spirit of resignation makes me have more merits, being neglected and ignored makes me a better man, humiliation makes me more pure, and the suppression of an explosion of anger makes me stronger. In other words, suffering endured with God makes my character deeper, more profound.

On every painting there is light and shadow; the talent of the artist is to blend these two opposites into a coherent whole. God, my Heavenly Father, knows about my troubles; if He allowed them they are part of His plan. What plan? How would I be able to comprehend that? He punishes me for my past? Prepares me for my future? Wants to purify me? Wants to make me more serious? Wants to give me opportunities to earn merits? I cannot possibly know this. But I know one thing: that I have to emerge from the fire of suffering better, purer, with a deeper and more serious soul.

My prayer will be the following six lines:

> Lord, Thy Will be done,
> Then be that as it may!
> Lord, Thy Will be done,
> Even if it hurts!
> Lord, Thy Will be done,
> Even when I don't understand!

Suffering endured without complaints is an excellent means of forming character and strengthening the will. Human nature tries to free itself from suffering, and if not successful, it finds relief in complaining and crying. However, if you marshal all your forces to accept your fate with a calm spirit, you have greatly strengthened your will power. If someone has a weak will, he will be pulverized by the hammer blows of suffering like a sand castle; by contrast, the manly character will become stronger under those same hammer blows like high-alloy steel. When Seneca said that someone can be a hero in the sickbed just as much as on the battlefield, he tried to say that the best test of the reliability of character is suffering. As Holy Scripture says: "For whom the Lord loveth, he chastiseth" (Heb. 12:6). On the marble statue of character the finest features are chiseled by suffering.

In your sufferings remember the words of Baron József Eötvös: "Whoever keeps his trust in Divine Providence even after suffering some losses will not be crushed by fate." His following words can be used as a prayer: "I leave to others the smooth roads on which one can travel far with little effort, and all the goods which the majority of people most desire. To me, Almighty God, give the thorny path that always leads upwards, where I will be always convinced not to lose my way." If the Roman said proudly *fortia agere Romanum est,* to do great things is a Roman virtue, you may extend it by saying *fortia pati Christianum est,* suffering with a great soul is a Christian virtue.

Just think a little how the souls of the most noble of pagans were engulfed by a nameless sadness, pessimism and despondency. I cannot think of any of them that did not prefer death to life. While luxuriating in sensual pleasures, it was the most noble souls who became disgusted with the world, not being able to see any lofty goal for this earthly life. Only one or two, having a presentiment of Christianity, could rise into a more purified, exalted atmosphere. For example, how devastatingly dark the furies are in the dramas of Aeschylus. The pagan, when he suffers, can only gnash his teeth in his suffering. The God-fearing also suffers, not with blind fatalism but with self-composure. Christianity cannot eradicate poverty, misery, suffering and sin either, but at least it is able to comprehend what God's purpose is with all these.

Do you have to suffer a lot, my son? Are you poor, ailing, your parents in poverty, suffer from adversity? What is the intention of God with you? Maybe He punishes old sins. Maybe He is softening your soul for a more zealous life. Maybe He is tempering your will like fire tempers steel. Maybe He wants you to increase your merits for eternal life. Maybe He is guiding you through life like a tourist guide.

"You led me through such rocky, hard, narrow, unpleasant roads!" cries the tourist. "Indeed, I led you through uncomfortable roads, but you know if I lead you on the wide and comfortable road, we shall end in the swamp and never get to the heights!"

"Why do I have to suffer so much?" you ask. Only God knows. But look at a beautiful Persian carpet: flowers, patterns, colors in an artful arrangement and artistic unity. Then look at the backside: total chaos of threads and colors. That is much like life. We only see the backside. The single great, comprehensive, central thought is in God's hand. The eternal God sits at the loom of history, and His intentions are incomprehensible to us. "For my thoughts are not your thoughts: nor your ways my ways, saith the Lord" (Is. 55:8).

> Stop, thou words on my lips!
> God knows what He does,
> His plans blind man cannot comprehend,
> And questioning Him is not permitted.
>   (Petôfi)

Saint Catherine of Siena (1347-1380) once had to struggle against an extremely violent temptation. When she finally conquered it, she complained sadly: "My Jesus, where were you when my heart was engulfed in darkness?" The Redeemer answered: "I was in your soul. Had I not been there with you, those thoughts assaulting your soul would have penetrated your will and would have caused the death of your soul." So do not be afraid of sufferings either. A single rock can break the force of the strongest sea waves.

So do not be like certain plants: while the sun is shining it proudly lifts its head, but when the twilight comes it pulls its petals together and wilts and droops sadly. Suffering is God's artwork on the marble of your soul. It searches for gold in your soul; gold is not on the surface, it has to be mined with great effort. The marble would like to cry out under the hammer blows of the sculptor. But if the sculptor would "spare" the marble, there would never be a beautiful masterpiece produced. You do not have to search suffering out, but when it comes, look it boldly into the eye:

So thank God when He tries you,
And thank Him when He eases up on you.
(Goethe)

Unconditional Obedience

Another tool of forming character is obedience. It is a difficult task in adolescence. But a little thinking in the age when you begin to use your mind should reveal that obedience is the essential foundation not only of your liberty but also of the life of society. It is a pleasing sight to observe a troop of boy scouts stepping together, throwing out their chests, and then a small "stop" command makes the whole troop stiffly come to a halt. What creates the pleasant impression? The organized obedience.

Why do you have to obey? First of all, because you are not an independent being. "What? I am not independent? What or who do I depend on?" Well, you depend on an untold number of things and people. You are not the center of the universe and cannot live as if you needed nobody. Do you know who could do that? Who gives birth to himself, who places himself into the crib, who suckles himself, who would grow as large as he desires, lays himself into the coffin, digs his own grave and buries himself. You laugh? That there cannot be such a man? Of course! Therefore, there is no completely independent human being.

Secondly, you have to obey because that makes you truly free. "On the contrary, it is disobedience that makes you free," you might think. Wrong. Disobedience makes you lawless, ungovernable and unmanageable. Just look at a horse that breaks out of harness and runs wildly around. Is it free? No, it is ungovernable. At the end it destroys itself.

Then you have to obey so that you may be able to command. Who is the person most likely to obey? Strong personalities. The more often our soul voluntarily yields to the just demands of others, the stronger

our soul will become. Over the road to freedom of soul we can read: Obedience. Goethe writes in *Iphigenia in Tauris* (V. 3.):

When I obeyed, my soul was truly free.

Obedience is an excellent means of strengthening the will. The young man must understand that those who command him, his parents and teachers, want to do things to his advantage, instead of merely irritate him. He must also understand that a boy of fourteen or sixteen years does not have the practical experience and the serious, full comprehension of life that his forty- or fifty-year-old father has. So if your parents or teachers give you orders, do them without murmuring even though you may think they are severe with you. Realize that you still lack experience, you are more careless, more strongly under the confusing influence of appearances and the blinding influence of the senses.

We never hear grown-ups complain that their parents were too strict with them when they were young. On the other hand, many remember their childhood with sadness, regretting that they did not obey their parents. My son, I hope you are obedient. Be so always not because you have to be, but because you want to be, because it is to your advantage. What you have to do, you should also want to do, and you will doubly benefit. Pray often the magnificent words of

Saint Augustine: Grant what Thou commandest and then command what Thou wilt.

Persevere without Lies

One more "perseverance" is awaiting you: persevere with the truth. Only man is able to speak. A parrot is able to imitate words spoken by human beings, but only human beings are able to form words. Man endowed with this special privilege has a resulting responsibility. If only man has the right to speak, then it is his duty to speak truthfully, to use words correctly. "But I say unto you, that every idle word that men shall speak, they shall render an account for it in the day of judgment" (Matt. 12:36), teaches the Lord Jesus.

And this Our Lord Jesus Christ not only taught, but He also gave examples for the correct use of speech. Read the Gospels to see how well considered and magnificently calm every word spoken by Our Lord was. Animals can only make noises: howl, whinny, screech or groan, empty shells without seeds in them. The human word is not an empty seed; it has content, it has meaning, it hurts or praises, it insults or cherishes, improves or damages. Words uttered carry enormous responsibilities. It is too early to speak about character in a person who does not consider his words before uttering them.

The ideal of Catholic education is the young man who can be polite without flattery, can be truthful without being rude, can be honest without being helpless, can be friendly without being unprincipled, and remain true to his principles without being offensive. The sun runs its shining, crystal clear course in the sky, there is no darkness, no secretiveness in it; faces light up when they look towards the sun, they find strength, joy and life in it. A man with a truthful soul is such a life-giving force in society, we look on him and count on him always with joy.

Can there be a greater praise of a young man than to be able to say: "He understands the responsibility of every one of his words. He is never careless with his words! You can count on what he says! He always speaks with charity, and always sticks to the truth!"

Why Do Young People Lie?

Mostly they lie out of fear. They have done something forbidden, and now they are afraid of the punishment. When in fact it is the greatest foolishness to redouble your original fault, and on top of the first sin–most of the time not even a sin but mere clumsiness (broken glass, spilled coffee)–pile on a second sin, a lie. It would be much like the young man who splattered mud on his clean clothes, but then to make the stain disappear he would roll in the mud.

It would make much more sense to say: "I did make a mistake. What if I admit it? I will get a scolding. After all, I deserve it. By to-morrow I will get over it, and at least I remain honest and truthful. If, on the other hand, I lie to escape punishment, I cause a much bigger wound on my soul, which will keep on festering and will never leave me peace. So, I should honestly admit everything. I am very sorry, Mother, I was clumsy (truculent, hasty), I will take better care next time. Please punish me..." Your honor has been saved, and after such an admission you may not even get punished. But even if you do get punished: "I should suffer for the truth rather than the truth should suffer for me."

Another lies out of cowardliness. The conversation is about se-rious principles, ideals, religion; some shallow young men begin to mock these things. Now is the time to stand up, to take sides, to give testimony to your principles, to give testimony to the truth, but no, you do not dare, you are afraid of ridicule, you are afraid of the mock-ing faces. You rather lie. You are a coward.

It is possible to lie out of envy or jealousy. Your schoolmate is be-ing praised. "Oh, he does not deserve it, he has all these faults..." you say and you lied.

It is possible to lie for the sake of advantages ("not true, it was not a goal," "no, not true, the ball has not touched me"). It is possible to lie because of badly interpreted loyalty, when you want to help your friend in trouble with a lie.

Bragging may lead to lies: "I had a car last summer, oh you should have seen it, how many things happened to me," but not half of it is true.

You lie in school if you rely on prompting; you lie if you copy someone's paper, you display something that is not yours. The young man of character should say: "I am much more proud than to get ahead by dishonest means."

There are young men who do not tell the truth because they are superficial. They do not mean to lie, they merely "babble"; but still they are unreliable because they are not used to being careful, not used to using their senses correctly (read the section entitled "Sanctuary Lamp of the Cathedral of Pisa" a few pages ahead).

Take care, my son, it is rather easy for a young man of character to stay away from the obvious, big, brutal lies, but the small lies and inaccuracies also damage character. An honest young man never says: "It wasn't me" when in fact it was he. But many are likely to say, "Sometimes I was among them" when they should have said, "Often I was among them." Or they say, "I will certainly go" when they should have said, "I will go if at all possible."

Everything is a lie that goes against truth and honesty. Therefore it is possible to lie not only with words, but also with silence, with hypocrisy, dissimulation, and duplicity. If you say half of what you should say, you lie; if you hem and haw, you lie; if one never knows where he stands with you, you lie. There is an enormous jungle of lies.

Is It Worth Lying?

Once I asked a young man: "What do you think, is it worth lying?" "No" he answered decisively. "Why not?"

"Because it will come to light sooner or later, and then there goes your honor." It is a good argument. Indeed, I can hardly imagine a more humiliating situation then catching a young man previously thought to be honorable in a lie. He has been found out!

Another one thinks: "If someone is clumsy he should not lie. There are ways to lie cleverly. You have to prepare it well, what you are going to say if they ask this, and what if they ask that; and that way you will succeed..."

But it will not succeed for long. "In vain does the donkey hide behind the door, his ears stick out..." goes the saying.

And the Latin saying warns the dishonest man: *Mendacem memorem esse oportet*–A liar needs a good memory (Quintilianus). Sooner or later the liar gets into a contradiction; he needs new lies to shore up old lies and so the lies multiply. Once he deviates from the truth, he is in a dangerous swamp where he is likely to sink. Sooner or later he will slip up, forget one of his lies and lose his honor. The lie is a monster born of moral failings, and monsters do not live long.

But just for the sake of argument let us assume that the lie does not come to light. He lied so skillfully that nobody found him out. Think how is it going to continue. When he is alone, there is an inner voice accusing him: "You are dishonorable! Nobody can trust you!" Such self-accusation brings very bitter moments to the most skillful liar. Woe to him who has given himself over to lying. The lie comes from deep darkness where Satan dwells, who brings darkness to the soul. Even his eyes betray the liar; he casts down his eyes, he is afraid that his eyes will give him away.

Read how Iphigenia complains in Goethe:

> Painful lie! It does not liberate
> Like other truly spoken words;
> It does not comfort us.

An interesting fact: today medical doctors are beginning to be somewhat more careful about prescribing poisonous substances as medicines; they are beginning to realize that the poison may cure one illness, but may cause another one even worse then the one cured. Similar is the case with lies: it appears that the lie saved you from some unpleasantness but it causes great damage in other respects. And even if conscience can be silenced, there will come the day, the Day of the Last Judgment, when all deceit, trickery and lies will be brought to light by the All-Knowing God, who cannot be deceived by even the most skillful liar, and about whom it is said, "Lying lips are an abomination to the Lord" (Prov. 12:22).

God is the living Truth, therefore every lie is the denial and distortion of our resemblance to the Divine existing in our soul. It is said about the fox that when it is entrapped, it is willing to chew off its own leg or tail to escape. If someone is trying to escape trouble by lying, he is chewing off not his leg but, what is much more important, his honor and character. Lying is cowardliness; sticking to the truth is heroism.

> The liar is a cowardly creature; A hero is he who always speaks the truth.

You achieved an advantage by lying? You paid for it very dearly. Lying got you out of some trouble? You got into a much worse trouble. You received some distinction in the eyes of others by lying? You lost your honor in your own eyes.

Ein Mann, ein Wort! (An Honest Man's Word Is as Good as His Bond)

But maybe there are cases when it is permissible to lie? There are boys who excuse themselves very quickly. "I lied for a joke! That cannot be a sin! I harmed nobody with it!" Not a serious sin, but still a sin. You may have harmed nobody else with it, but you harmed yourself. *Wer lügt, betrügt*–Whoever lies, is deceived.

The biggest problem with the so-called innocent lies is that they get you used to more serious lies. Great characters protect themselves from these with care. We find examples of this even among pagans. You have learned about Aristides (530-468 B.C.), the Athenian general and statesman, that he never lied, not even for a joke: *"Aristides adeo fuit veritatis diligens, ut ne joco quidem mentiretur."*

It is important to see clearly what a lie is. A lie is not telling the truth in order to mislead someone. So if one is merely playing, jesting, wants only amusement, then there is no lie involved. What is forbidden is to mislead others.

I admit that once in a while one may have to choose between a lie and a serious trouble. The principle must remain sacred and inviolable: "I will never lie!" On the other hand, there is the threat of serious trouble which will result from my telling the truth. What to do? A simple solution may be silence. We give no answer. The other side will realize that the question is troublesome for us, and he may stop insisting on an answer. If someone is clever one may give an evasive answer–evade, shirk, blur the issue, talk beside the point, find a plausible excuse or pass it off with a joke. But often these are not accepted, and then nothing else remains but to live with the troublesome consequences.

So, if possible, try to avoid trouble, but if that is not possible, *fiat iustitia et pereat mundus,* let there be justice, though the world perish. Consistently telling the truth is not easy, it is the virtue of heroes!

One easily forgives little children: they lie out of fear of punishment. They are far from having character. But what to say about older boys on their way to growing up, proud of their intellect, courage and honor; it is sad when they prove to be cowards and try to escape a well-deserved punishment with a lie.

How much more impressive is the character of the young man who never lies because he is simply not able to lie. He is candid, simple-hearted, to lie would do violence against him. How wonderful it is to meet such a young man on whose word one can always rely and build, whose words are true like Holy Scripture. *Ein Mann, ein Wort!*

God wanted to make it difficult for man to lie, so He made man in such a way that he blushes when he lies. It is possible to learn to lie without blushing ("as if he read it from a book"), but it is a cursed science! So, my son, be proud of your truthfulness! And every boy who cares the least bit about his honor, manliness and character should be veracious to the last word. The boy who lies easily attacks the foundations of his character, and inescapably heads for moral disintegration. Whoever violates the truth will not be faithful to his duties either. Whoever wants to get ahead with untrustworthy speech will be dishonorable in life too: he will be bribed as a public official, he will cheat as a merchant; whatever he is, he will have no character. Even if it may not be true literally, it is true substantially: "You start with lies, you end on the gallows."

The motto of the young man of character: Truth at all cost! Holy Scripture says: "If any man offend not in word, the same is a perfect man" (James 3:2). Denying the truth is the surrender of human dignity and the betrayal of our sacred human obligations. I know of no circumstances under which it would be permissible to lie and risk our veracity. Never! No need ever justifies it! I know that some boys try to say: "This time, I simply had to lie" but it is only an excuse. You never have to lie. If we just once concede the necessity of lies it means the end of law; from then on everybody can use it as a defense that "this time it was impossible to avoid lying."

What would happen to society if lies were tolerated! Nobody could believe another person. The boy could not believe his parents, the parents could not believe their children. Every moment I would have to say: this person is trying to cheat me. I would not dare eat my soup because it might have been poisoned by the cook. I would not dare call a doctor because he might try to kill me, *etc*. Life would become impossible. Lies are incompatible with human society.

Swear to It!

If someone always keeps his word, he will never need the life belt of infirm characters–rash and thoughtless swearing. "Are you coming to play ball this afternoon?" "I am coming." "Swear to it!" or "Can you lend me the dictionary?" "I can." "Swear to it!" And so on, irresponsible youths swear to hundreds of insignificant things.

Do not let this happen to you. It is much more responsible and manly behavior to say instead of swearing to the truth of things: "Boys! This is how it is! I do not lie!"

When I hear such unnecessary swearing, I always think: This boy lies so much that when he once tells the truth he knows nobody believes him, so he has to swear to the truth of his words. If someone does not lie, he does not need to swear. Always keep your promises, keep your word. Consider carefully what you are going to promise.

Do not promise anything carelessly. But once you promised something, you have to keep it at all costs. If they cannot count on your word under all circumstances, you are not a young man of character. *Falsus ore caret honore*–he who lies, slays his honor. If, on the other hand, you are always faithful to your promises, you display an impressive self-discipline. How could society survive with people who do not keep their word!

Ein Mann, ein Wort–An honest man's word is as good as his bond, says the old saying proudly. Very true! A man does not trifle with his words.

Whatever happens to you in life, you should have the consolation of French king Francis I (1494-1547):

> *Tout est perdu hormis l'honneur!*
> Everything is lost, but honor remains.
> *Omnia si perdes, famam servare memento.*

One more important thing to point out: you have to be honest not only with others, but also with yourself. No matter what you do, ask your conscience: Is it right to do so? But don't deceive yourself. If you dare to be honest with yourself, many times you will have to admit deceit: it was simply not true when you said "I had no time to prepare this homework"; what you claimed to be a generous deed was in reality selfishness; when you viewed that picture of a nude it was not true that you "wanted to study artistic beauty"; and when at that party you got involved with indecent speech it is not that "after all you are not a child any more," but you are indeed a coward who abandons his own principles.

Oh, if you could always be honest with yourself! Have frequent, quiet conversations with yourself to get to know yourself. And then admit to yourself that you are still young, so behave accordingly. Do not try to imitate grown-ups in their behavior or in their amusements. Do not pronounce pretentious judgments on things that you cannot yet sufficiently understand because you lack the required education and life experience. Do not think that you can understand everything, that you correctly understand them, and that you are allowed to read everything and allowed to imitate everything. You are still young, so believe that your true greatness resides in obedience. You are still young, so you cannot yet demand things that grown-ups have earned with hard work. You are not yet earning money, so do not spend money unnecessarily that others have earned for you. So you see in how many things you have to be honest!

And then you have to be honest with God! We are dependent on God in every one of our heartbeats, in every breath taken, in every glance of our eye. What a lie, what self-delusion for young men to believe that they have no need of God, that they are self-sufficient, and then live accordingly. Is it honest to have the Faith, to have religion but hide it and deny it? The dishonest youth easily neglects his religious duties during vacations, whereas the serious and devout has even more zeal for his daily prayers, for attending Mass, for approaching the sacraments, because he has more time during vacations than during the school year.

God Himself is eternal truth, therefore serving truth by always telling the truth is worship. Who openly and truthfully answers all questions glorifies God by his words; who serves some noble cause without any reservations in the back of his mind glorifies God by his deeds; whose life is an open book, honest, clear, unclouded like a mountain stream has God reigning in his life. See, my son, what great task is awaiting us: to be honest, thereby spreading the realm of truth, and thus preparing a dwelling for the God of Truth among men.

Just look around yourself to see what enormous amounts of lies are darkening this world! How much deception, how much eye-wash and window dressing, how much work for the sake of appearances, superficiality, cheating, trickery and fraud! All this is darkness, none of it is the kingdom of God. What could you do against these for the kingdom of God? Maybe preach against lying? You will not accomplish much with it. Rather be a fanatic devotee of truth, witness to the truth in your words, deeds and life, then everything you do will strike a blow for the kingdom of truth.

Aggredere! (Know How to Act!)

To the forming of character, *Abstine!*–know how to deny yourself!–is not enough; neither is *Sustine!*–know how to persevere!–enough. In addition, you also need *Aggredere!*–know how to act!

There are boys for whom self-denial and perseverance come rather easily, but they shy away from work that requires energy. That is not right. By young men of character we do not mean cowards who sit in the corner and hang their heads; by self-denial we do not mean ease and comfort; and by Christian life we do not mean rest and idle tranquility, but rather movement and activity since even the happiness of heaven is called "eternal life." Our religion not only has commandments saying what not to do, but also plenty of others that prescribe what we should do. Therefore, *Aggredere!* Act!

It is said that fate has an iron fist, it may strike down anybody. Never mind! You, on the other hand, have a soul and as a consequence have greater perseverance, resistance and resilience than the whole material world.

You need to put forth. You are going to have to put more effort forth if you want to succeed. The steel blade is firm yet elastic. How did it become that way? In fire, in hot flames.

Human life is a long sequence of tiny events. Each in itself looks insignificant, yet they make up life. Every skyscraper is built from many small structural components; life is made up of trifles, of mere nothings; and every great moral fall begins with some small moral lapse.

If someone is careful and prepared in small things, he is not in danger of a great fall.

If you fall while walking on the street, what is the most likely cause? Do you trip up over a big stone? No, you can see it from a distance. But you can trip and fall because of a small stony seed of a cherry. "Why do they bother me with such trivialities?" cries the boy when the command he received looks unimportant to him. But is it a triviality if in a complex machinery intermeshing gears do not quite fit together, if one is off by just a little? Is it a triviality if the note you play on the violin is off by a half note? Ask those who know about horses for fancy carriages, is it a triviality when of two beautiful black horses, otherwise identical, one has a white spot on his forehead and the other does not? A triviality may have enormous importance in the moral life. Napoleon had great talents and could have done great good to mankind. But he failed, and the cause of his downfall was a single fault, his immense vanity. The moral decay of many boys started with trivialities that at first appeared harmless. Not to observe one or two disciplinary rules of the school, to excuse their laziness with lies, squander afternoons in bad company: they do not appear so terrible at the first sight. But acts often repeated become habits: bad acts become bad habits, good acts become good habits. First it bothers him that for the sake of loudmouths he denied his serious principles, but "it was so good to be with them!" By the third or fourth time it is much easier and more comfortable to compromise on conscientiousness.

The Power of Trivialities

Where does the power of trivialities come from? Nothing in the world disappears without a trace. Even the most insignificant, paltry matter makes its tiny contribution to the great whole of life. One can get used to acting morally just as easily as to the sinful life. After many tiny noble acts it is just as easy to follow a noble life as after many sinful acts one may easily follow a sinful life. The more perfect something is, the more exact it is in the smallest details.

Men in olden times understood the world only in the broadest terms, yet what they knew forced them on their knees before their Creator. How much deeper our reasons are for paying homage to the Creator since we have telescopes and microscopes to penetrate the details of the universe, and we are speechless seeing the incredible accuracy of order, purposefulness and connections there. The precision of details in God's creation should be the example we follow in forming our character.

This being understood, no small detail will be insignificant any more for you. You can now see that observing accurately prescriptions that may seem insignificant have strong educational value (for example, fasting rules of our religion). Easy to find many other examples. If on a hike you can sit before a spring for fifteen minutes although you are very thirsty; if you can control your tongue not to relate immediately some interesting story eagerly awaited by your fellows; if while walking on the street and finding a big crowd not to go there immediately to investigate no matter how curious you are–with all these apparent trivialities you perform an important task of liberating your will from the bondage of instincts and passions.

But these also help you realize that when the Catholic religion speaks about self-denial and self-control it is not threatening human happiness, rather through them it helps you achieve the free life alone worthy of human beings, which is the freedom of the soul. One who does not practice self-denial cannot truly be religious; a truly religious person day by day conquers matter, conquers the body.

Baron Miklós Wesselényi (1796-1850), an Hungarian statesman, wrote: "Everything gets labeled great or small because of its effect and consequences, and if something has important and great consequences it is never small no matter how it appears." So by now you may believe that once a whole battle was lost because of a horseshoe-nail! The horse of the commanding general was missing a nail in his horseshoe, so the horseshoe fell off. Because of the missing horseshoe, the horse stumbled, and the commanding general fell off his horse. The enemy killed the general, and the whole battle was lost because a miserable horseshoe-nail was not fastened carefully enough!

Gulliver Tied Down

The path of the human soul is much like ice on the street. At first it is rough, not very slippery, but becomes smoother and smoother as boys slide along its full length more and more often. Eventually it becomes dangerously slippery. Similar is the case of human actions: the more often we do something, good or bad, the more we get used to it, and the more easily we repeat it, and by the end we are almost inevitably sliding in the often tried direction.

Do you know the story of Gulliver? When he is washed ashore after a shipwreck in the country of Lilliput and awakes to find himself prisoner of a race of people one-twelfth the size of normal human beings (six inches tall), he is tied down, his arms and legs, even his hair, with thousands and thousands of fine strings, against which he was defenseless.

You see, my son, this helps you understand why serious people try to eradicate even their smallest faults. If one yields to his disordered inclinations in little things, he will not consult his conscience in more serious things either.

And it is shocking how many young men entered the path of sin after growing up merely because in little things they started to be negligent and permissive. Such a young man grows up also, but only to become a caricature of a real man, much like a snow man, who resembles a man after all, with eyes, a mouth, and a paper hat on his head, except that he does not have a character and a strong will.

Seeing the desk or study of some students, I was alarmed: "Oh, my God, if in the soul of this boy there is a similar disorder!" Shoe brush and Latin dictionary, bicycle pump and math book, buttons and ruler, a dried piece of bread and tooth paste on top of each other in "poetic" disorder... You should have order on your desk, in your closet, in your room. Not only because the external order expresses the internal col-

lectedness, but also because it facilitates it; if your things are in order, you will find it easier to keep your thoughts in order too.

If your things are in order, you will find it easier to be on time; whereas many boys waste a lot of time searching for things making them late everywhere. You must know boys who are alarmed, at ten minutes to eight a.m., at not finding the German language book. They throw everything around, in vain. It is gone. Finally they find it next to the shoe polish. But by now it is five minutes past eight. They run, they are late, they get a citation for disorder. Later in life they will do the same, missing even more important things. As an M.D. they will kill a few patients because they forget something "insignificant" from the prescription; as a pharmacist they will prepare the wrong prescription because they have not examined the writing of the M.D. carefully enough.

And the disorder in their writing! Their books are full of disordered markings, scribbling, highlighting. When the accounting of merchants gone bankrupt is examined, most of the time they are found to be disorganized and neglectful. It would be interesting to examine the notes of students who fail their courses.

Take care, my son, so that your character is not fettered by bad habits, little negligences and slovenly work. Keep order in everything, even in the smallest things. Your pencil should be sharpened, you pen in working order. There should be nothing on your desk except what belongs there, allowing possibly for some decorations; everything should have its customary place, books, pens, rulers and paper clips, so that you could find everything there even in the dark. Take special care of things you have borrowed (books, dictionary, *etc.*); do not lend to others things you have yourself borrowed, do not wait to return them until the owner sends for it, *etc.*

The Bad Lock

French economist Jean-Baptiste Say (1767-1832) describes how much damage can result from a small negligence. On a farm, he writes, the gate of a pen had a faulty lock. It would have taken a few minutes of work to fix it, but "it is nothing" said the farmer. Occasionally, a chicken or a duck escaped. Once even a piglet got loose. Now, that was not to be tolerated! Everybody, the whole family, the gardener, the washerwoman, the dairyman took to their heels and ran after the piglet to get him back. The gardener spotted the piglet first. He can get ahead of him if he jumps over that ditch. He stumbled, sprained his ankle, and had to stay in bed for a while. The washerwoman, returning from chasing the piglet, found that all the clothes left drying over the fireplace were burnt beyond recognition. And the dairyman in his haste forgot to tie up a cow, which got loose and broke a leg. All this damage from a neglected, insignificant lock which could have been fixed for pennies.

Sometimes, the most insignificant thing can become decisive in our lives. Algae may be considered insignificant, but they stick to the hull of ships. When the sailors of Columbus started rebelling after a long and apparently fruitless journey, he tried to quiet them down by saying: Look, there are algae on the hull of our ships, land must be close!

Or look at the great musicians! How much they have to practice to remain in the best form. Franz Liszt said once: "If I do not practice one day, I notice it; if I do not practice for three days, my audience notices it."

And do you know what makes up the great white cliffs of Dover? Shells of marine organisms that can only be seen by microscope. And what makes the huge steam locomotives move? Little insignificant drops of water turning into steam. What a wonderful thing the telephone is! And do you know what was the first step to this great invention? An apparently insignificant observation of Luigi Galvani (1737-1798), who had been conducting experiments with static electricity. When Galvani dissected a frog and touched the leg of the frog with a metal scalpel, he saw the dead frog's leg kick as if in life.

So get used to not considering anything in your work insignificant.

Absalom's Hair

The title of one of the novels of B. M. Bjørnson (1832-1910) is *Absalom's Hair*. It describes people who get ruined not because of great character flaws but rather because they could not gain control over little, everyday problems. Whoever rules trivialities also rules big things; and whoever can make good use of the fleeting moments rules time.

How could one accomplish something big, if he does not care about little things?

So do strive to be perfectly exact and faithful in the smallest duties even if they appear insignificant. Let us assume that you live in a boarding school, and at six a.m. the bell sounds to awaken you and to get you out of bed. You could linger lazily for a few minutes in your warm bed, but do not do so. Immediately jump out of bed, and go to washing. Is this insignificant? It only appears that way. In reality, it is a great training of the will, and conquest over laziness.

Or, the time for studying has arrived. Do not yawn, do not stretch, do not pick and choose sleepily from your books, but instead a brisk, short prayer and then tackle the work! Is this insignificant? No. It is a conquering of the self, training of the will.

About the executed criminal even his mother did not know when he was a small child that he would end on the gallows. The first step to *delirium tremens* is the first glass of alcohol; the first step to the million-dollar fraud is the greed of the first card game; the first step to bill forgery is the first plagiarizing in school; and the first step to debauchery is the first pornographic picture looked at in school.

Only if he recognizes in himself the small disorder can we expect him not to tolerate the big ones. Only if he refrains from small lies can we expect him to stick to the truth in difficult situations. Only if he is honest in the smallest things can we expect him to be honest in the big things.

These are the words of Our Lord Jesus Christ: "He that is faithful in that which is least, is faithful also in that which is greater: and he that is unjust in that which is little, is unjust also in that which is greater" (Lk. 16:10).

So, by now, you understand the words of the great Saint Augustine:

If something is small,
well then it is small,
but to be faithful in something
small is tremendous.

When you start to learn fencing, it is slow at the beginning; you have to learn the elements of fencing: ways of cutting, stabbing, or slapping. You cannot play Beethoven sonatas on the piano unless you practiced scales and technical exercises for years prior. And when you look at the training of soldiers, you see that they have to learn military steps, ways to march, running, leaping, swimming, burden carrying, not to mention uses of weapons, all essential to become effective soldiers.

"We squander our property one dollar at a time, our life one hour at a time, our conscience get blunted by compromising in little things; and as science reveals that whole mountains are made up of the remains of little creatures not visible by the naked eye, so the greatest difficulties in our lives are made up of such trivialities that we can barely notice them" (Joseph Eötvös).

Sanctuary Lamp of the Cathedral of Pisa

The ability to observe is also considered a triviality by some; although it is an important means of acquiring knowledge, getting ahead in life, and also of the training of the will. Strive to learn to use your senses well, to move around in the world with open, observing eyes; in other words, deliberately develop in yourself the ability to observe. The eye only looks, the soul, on the other hand, observes, watches with attention. The American Indians from a few blades of grass stepped on could read a lot, could derive conclusions; medieval Arabic astronomers learned a lot about the stars even without telescopes; Chinese painters very accurately depicted every detail of the motion of a flying bird; all these had excellent abilities of observation. Presence of mind, ability to observe and decide are important qualities not only for crews of airplanes and submarines, but for all those navigating the sea of life.

Kim's game (originally described in Rudyard Kipling's 1901 novel *Kim* and used by boy scouts) is an excellent means of developing abilities to observe. It is described by Robert Baden-Powell, the founder of Scouting as follows: "The Scoutmaster should collect on a tray a number of articles–knives, spoons, pencil, pen, stones, book and so on–not more than about fifteen for the first few games, and cover the whole over with a cloth. He then makes the others sit round, where they can see the tray, and uncovers it for one minute. Then each of them must make a list on a piece of paper of all the articles he can remember... The one who remembers most wins the game."

Try it! At first, you probably cannot remember half of the objects. Another good practice of the ability to observe is for several of you to watch the same event and later (maybe one day later) to describe what you all have seen. Everybody will describe it somewhat differently. Or, you all stand in a line, and the first whispers a sentence to his neighbor adding "pass this on." By the time the sentence gets to the end of the line, it has become quite different!

This is the way to learn how weak our ability to observe really is. One cannot even remember things one sees every day. Ask your friend: have you seen a pocket watch? Oh, sure, every day. Well, then try to draw it, you cannot.

Me, cannot? Here it is! Then he draws it with two errors in it. On this particular pocket watch four o'clock is indicated with "IIII" which he writes with *IV*, and he writes *VI* for six o'clock when in fact on this watch there is a small second indicator in that place. We cannot trust our ability to observe!

Therefore, exercise yourself in careful observation. What wonderful opportunities there are in observing the lives of animals! How the squirrel breaks a nut, how the dog eats, how the cat eats, how chickens are fed, how birds of prey tear their victims apart, how a snail moves, how a snake moves, how a caterpillar moves, *etc.* You have seen a horse move: walk, trot, canter and gallop; but could you explain how differently he moves his legs in the different gaits?

If one is merely gazing stupidly, in vain does he travel around the world; it benefits him little because he is not able to observe. He looks but he does not see. Whereas the one able to observe can penetrate beyond the appearances. Being able to make sharp observations helped mankind to many great discoveries.

How many others before Newton saw an apple fall off a tree! Yet he was the only one who thought deeply about it, eventually discovering gravitation. How many saw steam coming out of a coffeepot. Yet it was only Denis Papin (1647-1712), a French inventor, who reflected on it sufficiently to be led to the steam engine.

Röntgen (1845-1923), a German physicist, found a contaminated photographic plate. Did he angrily discard it? No, he pondered on how light could have reached the well-enclosed plate. And he discovered Röntgen rays (today called X-rays) which go through solid objects, an achievement that earned him the very first Nobel Prize in Physics in 1901.

Royal Navy officer Captain Samuel Brown was pondering the problem of building the cheapest possible bridge over the River Tweed between England and Scotland. Walking in his garden, he noticed a spider's web between two bushes. Couldn't he do the same out of steel? And he designed the very first suspension bridge, opened in 1820.

British engineer Marc Isambard Brunel (1769-1849) found the inspiration for building tunnels in a similar way. He observed the shipworm, *Teredo navalis*, which has its head protected by a hard shell whilst it bores through ships' timbers. This inspired Brunel to build the Thames tunnel, the first tunnel successfully constructed underneath a navigable river and built between 1825 and 1843.

And do you know how Galileo (1564-1642) discovered the properties of the pendulum? In the cathedral of Pisa the sacristan poured oil into the sanctuary lamp hanging from the very tall ceiling. This had been done for hundreds of years, and thousands must have watched it before. Yet only Galileo pondered with care what he saw, and remarked, to his great surprise, that the sanctuary lamp took as many beats to complete an arc when hardly moving as when it was swinging widely. Galileo discovered the crucial property that makes pendulums useful as timekeepers, called *isochronism*; the period of the pendulum is approximately independent of the amplitude or width of the swing.

Eager Work

A first-rate tool of the development of character and of the school of the will is work, every day duty performed with joy and enthusiasm. The pagans considered work degrading, not worthy of a free man. Only Christianity gave honor to work by teaching that work ennobles man. Christianity pointed out the great character-forming power of work. Work greatly strengthens the will because it requires self-control, self-conquest and perseverance. If one has a strong enough will to work tenaciously and conscientiously, he will also be able to control his passions more easily than the lazy one, who performs his work only carelessly and negligently. Work helps preserve health of body and soul, whereas inaction enervates, softens and undermines the same. Persevering work makes one resolute, serious and patient. You would not believe, my son, how much your will is strengthened if you carry out your everyday tasks at school exactly, eagerly and always on time.

Always plan out your afternoon carefully, and when the time comes, no matter what other occupation offers itself, no matter how much the sofa calls, no matter what interesting reading you found, no matter how your friends are calling, everything is to be set aside. First is my duty! Take the book in your hand eagerly! Study with your soul in it! Duty performed with conviction greatly strengthens the will. But only true, serious work trains the will, not mere tinkering and waste of time. True work is a real victory over our caprice, fickleness and love of comfort.

So it should be your principle to perform all work as well as possible. If you have seen some of the great buildings of the European

Middle Ages, say Cologne Cathedral or Milan Cathedral, what is most impressive about them is the thought that all the workmen and artists involved, painters, architects, builders, sculptors, pulled all their forces together and gave their absolute best, a character-building work. Today? The work of people is quick, superficial, slipshod work, as expected of work performed for pay.

You will derive a lot of joy from performing even the most insignificant work cheerfully, with eagerness and with your soul put into it. What matters most is not how important the work is you have to perform, but rather how you perform it.

You may have heard about Thomas Carlyle (1795-1881), the Scottish writer and historian. His wife once lost her patience, sitting next to an oven baking bread for her husband, when the baking did not go well. "I have to waste my time with such insignificant work!" But she quickly changed her mind: "Didn't Benvenuto Cellini stay up all night when his famous statue of Perseus was fired in a kiln? What is the difference between Cellini firing his statue and a wife baking bread for her husband?" Yes, you can put your whole soul into baking bread, and a honorable man is the one who performs little tasks very conscientiously. What is doing at all, is worth doing well; and if you do not intend to do it well, do not even start it.

A friend of Michelangelo (1475-1564) was surprised during a visit that the painter was still doing the same old work. "Your work is not making any progress at all!"

"Oh, yes, it does. I have made many improvements: I took away something here; over there I have made a wrinkle more pronounced; I made this softer; I made that mouth more expressive."

"But all these are such small things!" wondered the visitor.

"Yes, they are. But the little things make up the perfect, and the perfect is not insignificant."

When I was in Milan, I went up to the top of the cathedral. The whole building is made of white marble. And even on the top of it there are very many marble statues, the beautiful statues of the saints. When it was built, someone said to the sculptor: "All this effort! Nobody is going to see these sculptures from down below!" The artist answered: "Nobody will see them from below. But God will see them!" God will see them, and for me that is enough! This is performing your duty with your soul put into it.

Performing your duty with your whole soul does form your soul, whereas work performed reluctantly and superficially damages it. The latter is worse than doing nothing because it deceives you into believing that you worked a lot.

The material the artist uses to create a masterpiece is the same as the charlatan uses to create grotesque caricatures. One can be a hero of work and shape his character thereby, or can be the slave of it and suffer under its yoke. Man was born for work; if I have to work, I should work cheerfully and it becomes much easier as a result.

Duty

Duty! A magic word! Fulfilling duty lifts nations and individuals to heights; neglecting duty can ruin nations and individuals. Nations fulfilling their duty withstand the onslaughts of history, those neglecting their duty get destroyed. In an old European church there is an interesting picture depicting various missions in life.

There stands the pope fully adorned saying:
"I teach you all."

There stands the emperor with crown and scepter saying:
"I govern you all."

There stands the general with sword and helmet saying:
"I protect you all."

There stands the farmer with his plough saying:
"I feed you all."

And at the bottom of the picture there stands the devil grinning:
"And I take you all, if you don't do your duty."

Deep meaning to the picture! It matters not whether you are the emperor or the farmer, as long as you do your duty.

This earthly life is like a play in the theatre, where God gives everybody a role to play. It matters not what role you have to play, only how well you play it. It is just like in the theatre: it matters not what role you have to play, only how well you play it. You may play the emperor and you will be jeered because you did not play well; or you may play a beggar and you will be applauded because you did play well.

I often hear students saying sadly: "I do not know what career to choose. Everything is full." Do not be afraid, my son, in every profession there is a great shortage of capable and diligent men who will do their duty conscientiously.

Doing one's duty shapes character most profoundly: to do everything that is expected of us, and especially to do what is not to our liking. Believe the poet: life is to be evaluated not by how many of your wishes were fulfilled in it, but rather how many of your duties you were able to fulfill:

> By no means believe, O man,
> That your true happiness
> Is the number of wishes fulfilled:
> Rather, it is the number of duties fulfilled.

Life spent without working is like a picture without its frame. In the First World War a reconnaissance plane with two men in it was hit just when they were returning home. The man who took the photographs was killed and the pilot was injured, but with his last efforts he successfully landed the plane on home territory. His last words to his fellow soldiers coming to his aid were describing in broken sentences the enemy positions, and he pointed to the camera held by his dead comrade. At noon, both were buried, and at the same time the enemy positions were taken. What heroes of doing their duty!

Today I Am Not in a Good Mood!

Study, work, and its success depend on the will and not on your mood! Yet how many boys excuse themselves: "Today I cannot study. I do not have the right mood for it, and without it there is no point forcing myself. Tomorrow I will work twice as much..."

Do not forget: work put off till tomorrow is much harder to do than it would have been on the first day. Fulfilling your duty should never be made to depend on your mood. Duty postponed becomes more oppressive by the hour, and it threatens to poison your whole life. If you owe, you should repay as soon as possible. Do not ever forget the simple rule: First comes duty, then comes play.

Many boys like to complain: they have bad luck, the teacher picks on them, nothing ever works out for them. When in fact their problem is this: for them, first comes play, then for a long time nothing, and at the very end comes doing their duty.

You must have heard a lot about the guard at Pompeii. When Mount Vesuvius erupted in A.D. 79, fast-moving currents of hot gas, steam, water and rock engulfed Pompeii. People were escaping in the middle of great confusion, whereas the Roman soldier stood on guard. In the chaos, they forgot about him. His duty tied him to this place, he did not move. The soldier stood there until finally he was burnt or asphyxiated. Modern excavations found him standing guard. His helmet, spear and shield are treasures of Museo Borbonico, and he rather died sticking to his duty that stain the honor of Roman soldiers.

Probably no military tasks await you in your life, my son, but the great task of life does await you! You do have duties to God, to your fellow men, to the Catholic Church and to your country. This may sound like a hard saying, but it is the only one that becomes an honest man: We are not in this world to be happy, to have as much enjoyment as possible, but rather to do our duty, to do whatever God expects of us. We must say what the Redeemer of the world has said: "My meat is to do the will of him that sent me" (John 4:34). There are young men who always wait for "a better mood" to start studying.

By contrast, Horace says:

If one starts a work,
he has already accomplished half of it;
And if one keeps putting it off,
he is like the farmer
Who is waiting for the flood to subside
while doing nothing about it,
But it does not subside and the waves
keep rolling inexorably.

Whatever exists in heaven and earth is subject to the Divine Will. The laws of Nature obey the Divine Will: the star runs its course, the moon revolves around the earth, not because they want to but because they have to. It is man only that is not forced to follow the laws of God. God gave man free will, so the will of man may oppose the Will of God, which is sin. But if a man wants to avoid his own eternal ruin, then he also has to follow the laws of God just like the last blade of grass or the last little bug. So you have to perform your least

and most insignificant duty with the greatest possible care so as to earn the praise a simple stonemason once earned: "Every brick he laid down showed he was conscientious."

Horatio Nelson (1758-1805), the great, victorious admiral of England, died with these words: "Thank God, I have done my duty!" Great consolation at the end of a life spent in work! May you, my son, be able to say the same!

Who Was Born Late

Hard to believe but true: If one does not work, he can never be happy. Work promises bodily health. If the plough lies in the corner, it becomes rusty, whereas if it is used, it shines brightly. The idle man also becomes rusty, whereas the eyes of the diligent man are shining brightly. The sentence of man cannot be changed: "In the sweat of thy face shalt thou eat bread till thou return to the earth, out of which thou wast taken: for dust thou art, and into dust thou shalt return" (Gen. 3:19).

Nature itself declares the same: Idle people tend not to live long, whereas those who worked all their lives reach the greatest age. Reluctance to work is a modern disease, which shows a lack of strong will. To be able to work, you need self-conquest, self-discipline–in other words, you need strong will. By his nature, nobody is a worker. Just as the law of gravitation pulls matter down, soft human nature tends towards laziness. If, however, you overcome laziness, you will later enjoy the blessings of work. The secret of success: always work eagerly! Some boys need several hours of preparation for half an hour of study. "It cannot be done today! I do not feel like it today!" Never mind! An energetic will is going to move you past this obstacle too. Just get started with that work! You will see that despite all resistance you will make a go of it. Of course, there are those who yawn for half an hour, stretching endlessly, dawdling before getting started thereby creating an atmosphere hostile to the work.

And keep order in your studying too! The ancients used to say:

Keep order and order will keep you.

The orderly performance of work has double value, whereas disorganized, confused work is the biggest waste of time. Biographers of famous men often write that every evening they planned out their following day. You also should prepare a plan for the next day. And then stick to it! For example: I come home from school at one o'clock, lunch, rest until 2:30, study until 5, play until 6, music until 7, then dinner, followed by reading and studying a language, at 9 p.m. prayer and retire. When the time comes, execute the plan without deviation! Relentlessly! Ignore the temptations about how much time there is still until tomorrow morning, and that the sun shines so beautifully outside. Never mind! First is duty! You will see that having such a plan will give you time for so much more than living in chaos. Life is short, there is so much to know, so manage your little time well. The English saying is very true:

Early to bed and early arise,
Makes a man healthy, wealthy and wise.

There was a student who was consistently late always and everywhere. He was never on time, ever. His schoolmates invented the explanation: "He was born five minutes later than he should have been, and ever since he has not been able to catch up." When he grew up, he was not of much use anywhere because he was always late. It is to be feared that he will miss heaven also. Not by much, of course, only by five minutes.

Our Clock Was Slow

A man arrives at the railway station out of breath: "I have to catch the express train to Vienna!" "It has just left" he hears the answer. "Terrible! What will happen now? I should have made it! This is a disaster!" laments the frustrated passenger. But he has no right to complain: The train was on time, but he was not. Just as in life in general: Things in life are always exactly on time, it is people who are late.

What is the meaning of punctuality? It is very simple: Stop everything immediately when its time is past, and start everything immediately when its time has arrived. If you obey this simple rule, you accomplish everything you have to, and do so on time. Being punctual starts early in the morning. It is time to get up: say six a.m. Realize: the time for rest has passed, so jump out of bed. If you do so, you will not have to complain: I am sorry but I had no time to pray this morning.

The time for studying has arrived. What an advantage if you can be punctual now, if you can realize that you have to act because its time has arrived, instead of stretching for half an hour and counting your buttons: start, not start, study, not study... If one is punctual, he does not forget his book and notebook when starting out for school; when he returns, he does not throw his things around the room so that later he shall have to apologize: "I do not know where I put them."

Punctuality! Such an unpretentious word, yet an inconceivably important means of forming character. To do our duty hundreds of times every day as demanded by our work; to be conscientious even in small things; to put our soul into our work even when nobody looks and sees it; is there a more effective means of developing moral greatness and becoming a whole man? According to the famous saying: Punctuality is the politeness of kings. Truly, we need a royal quality, greatness, courage, heroic perseverance to overcome obstacles and respond when duty calls so that we never evade it, and never try to find excuses for doing so.

We can trust one with the great tasks of life only if he is always in everything punctual. A punctual young man even has more money in his pocket even though he may get less money from home than the one who is always late. What is the explanation? The punctual lad spends it only when it is essential and buys what he got it for. The other, by contrast, buys everything he runs into in the stores.

Whoever values time is always punctual. If he does not make others wait for him, he shows thereby that he values the time of others just as much as his own. On the other hand, if someone is inexact and disorderly in the beginning, he gradually becomes untruthful and unreliable; if someone cannot be trusted with time, we assume he cannot be trusted with anything.

If someone is inexact, we cannot trust his word, and such a man harms society as much as an anarchist or revolutionary. On the other hand, the one who is punctual and exact has demonstrated his reliability, his will power, his character. It is very much part of good character to stick to your words once you said yes or no.

"Please, teacher Sir, our clock was slow," the student who is late excuses himself. When in fact he should say: "Please, teacher Sir, I was negligent and disorderly–that is why I am late."

"Our clock was slow!" Do you know what George Washington answered to one of his clerks who excused himself this way? "Either you get another clock, or I get myself another clerk."

There is much truth in the words of Lord Nelson: "I owe all my success in life to having been always a quarter of an hour before my time."

The Poor Student

Often I am in awe when watching the almost superhuman efforts some youths have to make to be able to continue studying. The parents tend to be poor farmers barely able to support their son. The boy is outstandingly diligent, wakes early in the morning to do his own studying, earns some money by tutoring others, has no breakfast, every day he gets lunch from a different merciful family, his clothes are shabby, his room is unheated in the winter. In school, an elegantly dressed student sits next to him, preening himself, eating his fancy lunch, while my poor student sighs: if only I did not have to struggle so much...!

In case you are one of these poor students, I would like to comfort you, my son: Do not be ashamed of being poor. Spending your school years in such struggle has great educational value. Your rich classmate who grows up in plenty, squanders his youth never to return in partying, entertainment or sports overdone. To the rich studying is a mere interference with more entertaining activities, whereas for the poor it is the hope of a better future. I know many youths who completely lack a serious approach to life exactly because of a youth spent in affluence. I do not deny: poverty may derail many talents, but it is also certain that many more talents are lost because of affluence. The rich young man has difficulty finding a goal in life to motivate him, whereas to the poor, life appears like a department store, his work and efforts may buy anything for him he desires. If eventually he succeeds, he will realize how much he owes to his deprived youth. The rich young man merely earns a diploma; the poor one with his youth spent in hunger and cold, acquires self-confidence, manliness, inventiveness and decisiveness.

The Greeks have a saying: "Work is the money for which the gods will sell anything." Andrew Carnegie lists a number of American industrialists who started their careers as simple workers without any money (Wanamaker, Claflin, Lord, Field, Barr, Rockefeller, Gould, Seligmann, Wilson, *etc.*).

James Garfield (1831-1881), the twentieth president of the United States, was so poor in his youth that at the age of sixteen, when he yearned to go to sea, to earn the money for it he wanted to do some farm work. The farmer to whom he applied was inclined to reject him: "It is harvest time, and this work is for grown-up men, not for boys." "And if the boy can do the same work, is it not just as good?" asked Garfield modestly but with self-confidence. The farmer liked his answer and hired him.

Next day Garfield was sent into the harvest with four grown-up men. The four men dictated a fast pace to tire him out.

But the boy kept up with them, and by the time lunch had arrived the grown-ups were glad to be able to take a rest. The hands of Garfield were full of blisters, but he did not complain. After lunch he asked to be allowed to lead to show the farmer that he was able to work just like the others. The others agreed, but later they were sorry about the decision. Garfield dictated such a furious pace that the other men were exhausted by evening. Garfield did not appear to be tired, and when the others had retired he asked for a candle from the farmer.

"What is that for?" asked the farmer. "I would like to study a little; during the day I have no time for it." "But boy, you have done the work of three today, go to sleep. What is your name?" "James Abraham Garfield," he answered, and went upstairs and spent half the night studying. And he became the president of the United States.

I could give many other similar encouraging examples.

Poor Boys–Great Men

Stephenson, inventor of the railway locomotive, was born to parents who were both illiterate. His father was the fireman for the pumping engine of a coal mine, earning a low wage, so that there was no money for schooling of their boy. George was a brakeman for the coal mine and made shoes and mended clocks to supplement his income.

Watt, inventor of the steam engine, supported himself by an instrument-making business, later by being a surveyor.

Herschel (1738-1822), the outstanding astronomer, was also a musician. He played the violin, cello, the oboe and also the organ. He was first violinist in a Newcastle orchestra, and for years he was also a church organist. He composed many concertos, as well as some church music. Apart from a few oboe concertos, his music is largely forgotten today.

Benjamin Franklin (1706-1790) supported himself with work in several printer shops.

Antonio Canova (1757-1822), the great sculptor, was a stonecutter, just like his father and grandfather.

Tintoretto (1518-1594), the last great painter of the Italian Renaissance, was born as the eldest of twenty-one children. His father, Giovanni, was a dyer, or *tintore;* hence the son got the nickname of Tintoretto, little dyer, or dyer's boy.

Giotto (1267-1337) was a shepherd boy.

The father of Austrian composer Joseph Haydn (1732-1809) was a poor wheelwright. Haydn had a difficult childhood, he remembered being frequently hungry as well as constantly humiliated by the filthy state of his clothing.

Michael Faraday (1791-1867), famous English chemist and physicist (or natural philosopher, in the terminology of his time), was the son of a blacksmith. At fourteen he became apprenticed to a local bookbinder and bookseller, and continued doing that for seven years.

Pierre-Simon Laplace (1749-1827), French mathematician and astronomer, was the son of a farm-laborer and owed his education to some wealthy neighbors who liked his abilities and engaging presence.

What uplifting examples these are, showing that real talent, industry and zeal break through all obstacles and their strivings are unstoppable. Some more examples:

The father of the Hungarian poet and Benedictine monk Gergely Czuczor was a serf.

The father of Mihály Tompa (1819-1868), Hungarian lyric poet, was a village bootmaker.

The father of Mihály Vörösmarty (1800-1855), Hungarian poet, was a steward of the Nádasdy family. The death of the elder Vörösmarty in 1811 left his widow and numerous family extremely poor. Young Vörösmarty earned his living by tutoring.

József Katona (1791-1830), Hungarian playwright and poet, helped his father, a poor weaver, in his work.

Nowhere are better opportunities provided for the success of real talents than in the Catholic Church. It is well known that people holding the highest ecclesiastical offices often come from the talented sons of simple, poor families.

George Martinuzzi (1482-December 16, 1551), Hungarian statesman, a monk, an archbishop of Esztergom and cardinal, was from a poor family.

Vitéz János (1405-1472), the archbishop of Esztergom (1465-1472), was born into a poor Croatian family.

Szelepcsényi György (1595-1685), prince primate of Hungary (1666-1685), was from a poor Slovakian family, and he was educated at the expense of Pázmány Péter.

The father of Szcitovszky János (1785-1866), prince primate of Hungary (1849-1866), was a poor teacher.

Csernoch János (1852-1927), prince primate of Hungary (1912-1927), was born into a very poor Slovakian family.

Pope Saint Gregory VII (1020-1085), one of the greatest popes, was said to be of humble origins; he was the son of a blacksmith.

Pope Sixtus V (1521-1590) was Pope from 1585 to 1590. He was reared in poverty. His father was a gardener and it is said that, when a boy, he was a swineherd.

Pope Adrian VI (1459-1523), pope (1522-1523), his father was a carpenter.

What was their secret? Their talents? That too. But most importantly their iron will, perseverance, industry and that they used their time well.

What Is Time Worth?

There is an English saying known all over the world: time is money. In fact, time is even more than money, it is the fabric of life, from which life is made. If you want to get anywhere in life, you must know the value of time.

Time is becoming increasingly important in our life, so much so that only in small villages can people afford, before conducting their business, to have a civilized conversation about the weather, about the crops, and about the health of their families.

In the bazaars of Eastern countries it is customary for the merchant to talk much, recommend his wares, flatter the customers, make bold statements ("this costs me more than that," "I cannot possible go lower than that") so that the sale could have been completed ten times already in that amount of time. In more advanced countries discussion is kept to a minimum, and in American business establishments one can even read a sign like the following:

> When you have done your business, please trot.
> We know all about the weather.
> We have read all papers.

When I see in libraries the volumes Saint Augustine (354-430), Saint Bonaventure (1221-1274) and Saint Thomas Aquinas (1225-1274) wrote, I always wonder how did they have the time to write all these volumes when some of them died rather young, and writing was not the only thing they did?

For example, Saint Thomas Aquinas wrote twenty-four large folio volumes, when he only lived forty-nine years, and he taught and preached a lot in addition to writing. And he did not write light novels but discussed difficult problems of theology and philosophy. How did he find the time? He used well every minute of his life. If one wants to accomplish great things, he must be well organized in the smallest things. The secret of these men was: they made good use of their time.

Tempus omnia fert, sed et aufert omnia tempus. Time brings everything, and takes everything away.

To make good use of every minute is an important science. The old monk was right who wrote on the hour-glass of the monastery of Hamersleben the following warning:

> The past has flowed away, the future has not yet come;
> The present is turning on a point, and that is all you have;
> You have that point that is the present, use it correctly;
> a reward awaits virtue, and punishment awaits vice.

By contrast, those who "do not have time" for work are the ones who generally do nothing. The lazy student leaves everything to the last minute, and he writes his test-paper the night before it is due. And who are the ones who work most for the common good, who write the best scientific papers? Those who are well-off, who have no material cares, who have lots of time on their hands? Certainly not. Rather those who are busy from morning till night with work anyway. Indeed, the value of time is very great.

20 Minutes = 12 Million Dollars

How much is time worth? Apparently, 20 minutes are worth 12 million dollars. How so? The train between New York and Buffalo originally had to go around a deep valley of Tunkhannock Creek in Nicholson, Wyoming County, Pennsylvania. Between 1912 and 1915 it was decided to revamp this winding and hilly system. The rerouting was built between Scranton, Pennsylvania, and Binghamton, New York, resulting in the Tunkhannock Viaduct (also known as the Nicholson Bridge). The construction then cost 12 million dollars and it saved the train 20 minutes of traveling time. So for 20 minutes they paid 12 million dollars!

So very true is the following saying, even if Mephistopheles, the demon in the Faust legend, says it:

> Use the time, which so quickly passes,
> Order teaches you how to gain time.

It is especially important to use the time of our young age well for work and study because this is the time for accumulating knowledge and intellectual capital, the time for preparing for life. For the rest of your life, you will have to live on what you accumulated in your youth.

Life insurance companies are willing to insure young men not yet twenty for their old age for a small amount of money, knowing that a small amount saved in youth will grow large over the years. The same holds for intellectual capital accumulated during youth. For example, if you learn German at the age of forty, according to reasonable calculations you will be able to use it for twenty more years; however if you learn it at age twenty, you will be able to use it for forty more years; thus you will have it at your disposal for twice as long, just when you need it the most, for example, when you choose a career. It will open you more possibilities in life for a longer time.

My son, it depends on you what capital you accumulate for yourself! Everything you accumulate in your youth will pay off richly later in your life. The human body is arranged in a similar manner. You need physical education in your youth much more than later in life. But you are not able to study later in your life as effectively as in your youth. If you have not finished your studies by age twenty-four or twenty-five, you will never finish. Your ability to study decreases past the age of twenty-five; after that your intellect wants to produce rather than to receive. So if you have not learned something thoroughly by the age of twenty-five, you are not likely to learn it well later.

I am not advocating that young people overwork themselves. Yes, we need rest and recreation too, all in its own time. But do not try to mix work and recreation, because both will be harmed. Your motto should be: when you work, work hard; when you rest then laugh and enjoy yourself, do not even think of work. But never give time to daydreaming and idleness.

Transeunt et Imputantur

In days of old, it was a popular thing to do to write wise sayings on grandfather clocks to warn of the transitoriness of time. On one such clock we could read: *Transeunt et imputantur*, whose meaning is approximately: every minute passes, one after the other, but you have to give an account of each. One can almost see the endless line of agile minutes rushing by, and one can almost feel the breeze of mortality touching one's face.

Transeunt et imputantur! It would do a lot of good for many youths to remember this warning. There are many who have literally perfected to an art the wasting of time, forgetting that it is in their youth that they have to accumulate treasures for their life.

> Work is the salt of life
> To preserve it from decay;
> Idleness is never followed by
> blessings and success.
> (Mihály Tompa)

There are times in the life of a young man when he easily becomes a dreamer. He writes poems about the moonlight, always dreaming about the future, his imagination works out colorful varieties, while serious work gets neglected. Of course, work requires a lot more will power than novels sketched out by the imagination. Such dreaming boys weave the story of one of their favorite novels (how they imagine the continuation), they whisper gentle words to their hero, while time passes inexorably.

In the words of Mihály Vörösmarty:

> Daydreaming ruins life.

Is it to be wondered that it is so hard to return from the sentimental world of imagination to the serious and responsible world of carrying out our work and doing our duty? And he absolutely has to work, he does so reluctantly, without vigor. For such is the warning especially fitting: *Transeunt et imputantur!*

When the Past Becomes Present

Why are you not allowed to squander your free time on idleness or useless entertainments? Simply, because your time, your earthly life does not belong to you! It was lent to you, and some day you have to give an exact accounting of it. When exactly? You do not know. The only thing you know is that your death may come at any minute, and then God will open the great book of accounting, and then your past will become present. So be prepared for this accounting any moment!

It is salutary to think about this great accounting once in a while. "But I am so far away from it," you might say. You may well be far from it, but getting closer by the hour. And how far are you? Who knows? The old man has to die, the young man may die. I have seen young men of age 12, 15, 18 and 20 dead.

Imagine a very learned doctor examining you with great care, then declare solemnly that you only have eight days to live. Tell me, what would you do? How would you use your last eight days? Wouldn't you need to set things right?

To cleanse your soul? Ask many for forgiveness? To remove many faults from your soul? No matter who you are, you would make a very good use of those eight days. Experience fully supports the saying: *Heute rot, morgen tot!* Alive today, dead tomorrow.

Read how the great Michelangelo (1475-1564), with so many great masterpieces to his credit, complains in his old age about the wasted times of his life:

> Alas, alas, for I have been betrayed
> By fleeting Time and by the frank mirror
> Which tells the truth to our fixed glance displayed.
> So it befalls: he who commits the error
> Of delaying too much to the end
> As I have done (for my time has flown away)
> Finds himself, as I do, old in a day.

Nor can I repent, or prepare, or defend
Myself with death so nigh.
My own self-enemy am I
Uselessly pouring tears and sighs to my own cost
For there is no harm like time lost.

(*The Complete Poetry of Michelangelo*, translated by Sidney Alexander [Ohio University Press, 1991], p. 56)

Or read the same thoughts as expressed by Rückert (1788-1866):

Time never stands still, the moment flees.
When you do not use it, you did not live it.
If you never stand still, you never remain the same,
And he who does not improve himself, becomes worse.
He who does not make use of each day,
has done damage to the world,
Because he neglected to do what God had assigned him.

We read on an old clock: *Vulnerant omnes, ultima necat*–Every hour wounds, the last one kills.

Just think about it: how short human life really is. [The numbers of this paragraph originate approximately from 1927, when the world population was two billion souls.] Thirty years are taken to be the typical duration of human life. A drop in the ocean of time. A quarter of all children born die before reaching the age of 7; half of them do not reach the age of 17; one in a hundred reaches the age of 60, and one in five hundred reaches the age of 80. Every day about 120,000 people die in the world (even when there is no war); that means every hour 5,000 people die, and every minute 83 people die. Stop and think seriously: day and night, 83 people die every minute! So are you allowed to idle away your precious time?

Snatch as much time as possible from being lost! The words of Seneca the Wise sound disconsolate: "Most of our lives are spent in doing evil, a large part of our lives are spent in doing nothing at all, and our whole life is spent in doing nothing that we ought to do."

You live wisely if you remember that you are dying all the time. What a serious thought! In vain would you pull back the hands of the clock; death is also pulling in the other direction except with much greater force, so time flies. Our past already belongs to death. How old are you, my son? Sixteen? You see, sixteen of your years already belong to death. And what do you have left? Who knows except the Almighty? Therefore grasp the hours that belong to you. The past is not yours any more; the future is not yet yours; the only thing yours is the present moment–use it! It is still up to you to be able to remember with satisfaction in your old age your young years spent in honest work.

> Use the precious time while you can,
> The days, once past, never return.
> (Gergely Czuczor)

Young men often treat their time in a wasteful manner. "There is so much of it," they say. When they think of all the possibilities of the life before them, they become careless and thoughtless, they become elated as if seeing the ocean for the first time. Yet even the ocean has shores, and no matter how young you are the ocean of your life is not inexhaustible.

Non Numerantur...

Of all the time, only the present moment is ours, so let us use it well.

> Triple is the pace of time:
> Tarryingly approaches the future.
> Swiftly vanishes the present moment.
> Forever still stands the past.
> (Schiller)

Our clocks really mislead us: they always show time as if starting from some beginning, making us forget that time never returns. You may have a single moment in your life not used well that may have a decisive influence on your life. If the local train you are traveling on is late just one minute, you may miss the connection to the express train.

The servant says about his master idling away his time in his bed: "My master loses an hour each morning, and then never finds it again the whole day."

"Lived twenty years," I read on a tombstone. "What a short life," says somebody next to me. Short life? Oh, no. If he really lived twenty years, and used his life according to God's Will and he used his time well, in his few years he lived a full life.

God does not count the years but weighs them.

What is the secret of long life? How can I live a long life? People eagerly read books about such subjects. It is commendable to try to extend our earthly life. You also should do everything to protect your own health. But do not forget the most important thing: the longest earthly life is over quickly; so the wisest thing to do is to live a moral life and thereby gain eternal happiness. If you remember your mortality, you will not be reckless and squander your life. If you consider your death, you will become serious. Before death fades all vanity, folly, greed and anxious worry.

> Dying is the greatest deed of everybody,
> Dying is the hardest of all fights;
> The greatest deed: it earns the greatest wage,
> The hardest fight: it gives the most beautiful crown.
> (Weisz, *Lebensweisheit*)

The thought of death is sobering; we put down our pen, wipe the sweat off our brow and ask: "My God! What is the point of all this bustle, all these worries, when at the end it is the grave that awaits us?" And then you remember the consoling teaching of Our Lord Jesus Christ about eternal life.

> The thought of death makes selfish,
>   unscrupulous ambition turn pale,

but it does not paralyze all human efforts,
dying will always be conquered.

Whoever expects life beyond the grave faces death bravely because he knows that although everything passes, the value of a virtuous life remains forever–*omnia cum pereunt, est virtus sola perennis.*

Eternal life barely casts its first rays on the dying, and he already sees his earthly life in an entirely different light! If only nobody would ever have to say this one terrible sentence with his dying lips: "I lived in vain! Entirely in vain! All my life I chased perishable, contemptible vanities and now I have to go before the just Judge with empty hands."

Many people bewailed their lives in their last moments and cursed the recklessness of their youth; but never have I seen a single one who would have regretted that he lived his life as a dutiful, obedient, religious son of his Creator.

Ars Longa, Vita Brevis

This saying is strikingly appropriate: *Ars longa, vita brevis*–Life is short, but to learn a profession (an art) takes a long time. And it is becoming more and more true by the day: the realm of intellect is extending by great strides. There is more and more to know, and to acquire all that knowledge the duration of a human life is not enough. "If that is so, then it is best not to study at all," says Lazy Joe. The exact opposite is true! Because there is so much treasure to mine, use your time wisely, use every minute of it. A lot can be accomplished in a seemingly short human life, if you manage your time well. How many times people say, when they have a spare ten or fifteen minutes: "This period is so short it is not worth starting anything!" Yet, if they did not waste it, but put it to some use, they would gain many hours or days or even weeks just within one year. Not to mention a whole lifetime!

You do not know how much total time is available to you in your life, which should urge you to make use of the smallest interval. If you use your time well, you will never say there is no point in starting anything in the next fifteen minutes.

Goethe is right:

> It is better to do the smallest thing in the world
> than to regard half an hour as a small thing.

I read about a writer that his wife was always fifteen minutes late with preparing breakfast, and he wrote one of his books in those fifteen minutes. "Time is money." To make good use of small fragments of time, five- or ten-minute intervals, you have to be not only clever but you have to have strong will. You do not need strong will to say in September generalities like "starting next May, I will be truly diligent." You could put your time fragments to use by studying a language, for example. You will see how much progress you make in a few months by studying a language fifteen minutes a day.

You could put small time fragments to use by some work that does not need great concentration of attention, for example, writing letters or arranging your lecture notes. If you have to use mass transportation, you can do some light reading there. I have even seen young men, university students, studying anatomy, English words or mathematics on buses. Excellent! You can save a lot of time this way that would go to waste otherwise.

Quieti, Non Otio

Of course, rest and recreation are also needed to distance yourself from work. The bow always stretched taut loses its strength and flexibility. But rest should be regaining your strength, and not idling your time away. One can only rest if he worked before. If you "rest" without having worked before, you are merely indolent and slothful.

The Romans wrote over the entrance of their summer home:

> *Quieti, non otio.*
> Rest, not idling.

Rest and idleness exclude each other. Your mind should be occupied with something at all times. During summer vacation you may leave mathematics and trigonometry alone, and you may stop reading Thucydides (ca. 460–ca. 395 B.C.), Euripides (ca. 480–406 B.C.), Tacitus (A.D. 56–117), and Sallustius. However! Read what the German poet says:

> One can do something while resting,
> One can rest while doing.
>   (Logau)

Even if you do not live in the mountains, you can still enjoy refreshing excursions. If you are the member of a well-run boy scout troop, their camping could be a valuable part of your vacation. Try to occupy yourself with some manual labor or some skill requiring your hands. So, walking, hikes, manual labor and reading are all excellent ways to use your time during vacation. No matter what you do, you should never be bored.

Interesting to observe that boredom is not only a danger to the soul, but also to the body; laziness is more harmful to the body than work is, so if you are bored you are likely to shorten your life.

Also, when do people commit most murders, when are they most likely to get into fights? In their spare time, not during their work. You must have experienced this yourself: During the school year when you are busy with work, it is much easier to stay away from bad thoughts and from sin than during vacation when you have little to do.

Interestingly, the German language uses the same word, *"faul,"* to express decayed, rotten or putrid on the one hand, and lazy, idle and indolent on the other. As if to say: whoever is lazy, his soul begins to rot. Never to be doing nothing was the wonderful motto of Sir Walter Scott.

Students can hardly wait for the arrival of the great summer vacation, and those who worked hard for ten months, are in need of it. After all that studying you are at last allowed not to study, you are allowed to sleep a bit longer, but you are still not allowed to stay in bed lazily. The soul is always alert, producing thoughts; and if it cannot produce good seeds, it will produce thistles and weeds. The human soul works like a mill; if you pour good seeds into it, it will produce white flour, but if you do not pour anything into it (you are idle), it will grind up itself.

Remember the advice of Saint Jerome (347-420) to the young Nepotian:

> The Devil should always find you working,
> and then you have nothing to fear.

If in a garden ordinary plants grow, weed growth is less pronounced, as compared to a more neglected garden. The fewer useful plants grow in a garden, the more weeds are likely to grow in it. Similarly, if on a vacation you "do nothing," "weeds" and corruption will emerge in your soul.

Vacation is an excellent time for reading. What I recommended in my book *The Educated Young Man* you can never realize more easily than during vacation.

Vacation is also a great test of the strength of your religion. What you do during vacation will prove just how serious you are about religion. During school year, you had to participate in the religious activities of your school, obligatory student Masses, prescribed confessions, *etc.* By contrast, during vacation nobody urges you to do anything, nobody checks up on you. If you neglect your religion, it does not speak well of your character.

So vacation time is a valuable time, even though you are not studying. But this is only an appearance. During autumn, it looks like the tree is not working even though it is gathering strength for the following spring. Vacation is a comparable preparation for the following school year.

What Is Hardest in the World?

We smile when we look at an old map. In those days, large parts of the earth were unknown. With fabulous confidence, the makers of these maps marked the unknown regions with the sentence: *Hic sunt leones!* Here lions live.

Indeed, there are many students capable of rattling off the different kinds of metals found in the Rocky Mountains, or the kinds of indigenous people living in the Congo, but know little about the value of their own soul and know nothing about the wild passions ravaging their soul.

Already the pagan Pythagoras urged his students to put the following three questions to themselves twice daily (morning and afternoon): "What have I done? How? Have I done everything I had to do?" Sextius (ca. 50 B.C.) asked the following questions: "What weaknesses have you healed in yourself today? What faults have you conquered? In what way did you become better today?" The pagan Seneca wrote: "It is my habit to examine myself every day. When we turn the lights off in the evening, I go over the whole day and put every word and deed of mine on the scale."

You can control yourself only if you know yourself. The driver of a railway locomotive is master of his machine only if he knows intimately all the details of its operation. Do you know why people do not like to look into their own soul? They are afraid of what they will see there, the faults, the weaknesses, the selfishness and the lack of love. Such things must have happened to you already. You have done something or you have said something for which people praised you, when in fact you knew you did it because of selfishness, or you did not do it because of stubbornness, or you said it because of vanity. If you do not know yourself, you always put the blame on somebody else. "Well, I do not have any luck," says a boy after getting a failing grade, when in fact he should have said: I lack diligence. Another one says: "At home they always torment me," when in fact he should have said: I was moody and insufferable.

It was for a good reason that the following was inscribed in the forecourt of the Temple of Apollo at Delphi: "Know thyself!" When the Greek sage Thales (624-546 B.C.) was asked what is the hardest thing in the world, he answered: "The hardest thing is to know yourself; the easiest is to revile others."

To get to know yourself is a difficult, but indispensable task! So often pose yourself questions like the following: What is my nature really like? What kinds of desires and aspirations manifest themselves in me? Others like this book, this song, this music; what do I like? Soft or loud? Solemn or cheerful? What am I like in society? Shy? Clumsy? What do I spend my time on most readily? Is it worth spending so much time on? What did God create me for? He specified an end for everybody, what is mine? What special talents or inclinations did He give me? What do I take most pleasure in doing? What do I succeed in doing most often? What are my virtues, good properties? Why so few? I could have more, it only depends on me. What are my chief faults? Why so many? I could have fewer, it only depends on me. *Etc., etc.*

Tell me what impresses you, what you admire, and I tell you who you are. If you admire rich people, you have a materialistic bent of mind. If you admire people in high positions, you are vain and ambitious. If you admire honest people of character, you yourself are one of them.

If, as a young man, you frequently pose such questions to yourself, slowly, over the years you begin to understand yourself, and when the time comes, choosing a career will not be difficult either.

All Right?

On great ocean liners, when night falls, a sailor climbs up to the top, his eyes scanning the horizon and then in a measured voice he declares: All right! You may all retire now. You should do the equivalent in your nightly examination of conscience.

When attempts are made to make use of static electricity or electric charge, the system must be isolated so as not to lose the accumulated electric charge by discharging it. The soul must also be isolated from the impressions reaching it from the world, so that in the evening it can be calmly examined. In the evening before retiring, stop in the middle of your evening prayer and run down the events of the day. Ask the questions: Is everything all right? What have I done today? What have I failed to do that I should have done? Have I done everything well? And if you find that here or there you have made mistakes or committed a sin, lift your eyes to our Crucified Lord and say: Lord, I have erred. Forgive me. It will be different tomorrow.

Benjamin Franklin (1706-1790), the great son of North America, inventor of the lightning rod, tried to remove every little fault from his soul with great seriousness. He understood well that little things have great power over us, so he prepared a table which helped him to check himself, his deeds of the day, rejoice over his victories and bemoan his failures. He distinguished thirteen virtues, as to which he always checked himself. These were:

1. **Temperance**.
2. **Silence**. (Speak not but what may benefit others or yourself; avoid trifling conversation.)
3. **Order**. (Let all your things have their place; let each part of your business have its time.)
4. **Resolution**. (Resolve to perform what you ought; perform without fail what you resolve.)
5. **Frugality**. (Make no expense but to do good to others or yourself; *i.e.*, waste nothing.)
6. **Industry**. (Lose no time; be always employ'd in something useful; cut off all unnecessary actions.)
7. **Sincerity**.
8. **Justice**.
9. **Moderation**. (Avoid extremes; forbear resenting injuries so much as you think they deserve.)
10. **Cleanliness**. (Tolerate no uncleanliness in body, clothes, or habitation.)
11. **Tranquility**. (Be not disturbed at trifles, or at accidents common or unavoidable.)
12. **Chastity**.
13. **Humility**.

"I wished to live," he wrote about himself, "so as never to commit any mistakes; I decided to fight all frailty....Because I knew, or at least

I thought I knew what is good and what is evil, I could not imagine why I could not always do the good and always avoid the evil."

He was very strict with himself; every day recorded little crosses in his table indicating that he erred against a certain virtue. The summary of a week might have looked like this table:

	Sunday	Monday	Tuesday	Wednesday	Thursday	Friday	Saturday
TEMPERANCE							
SILENCE	■	■			■		
ORDER	■■	■	■		■	■	■
RESOLUTION					■	■	
FRUGALITY		■				■	
INDUSTRY			■				
etc.							

Couldn't you also implement for a few years this excellent method of self-education? But even if you find recording violations in tables tiresome, at least never omit the daily examination of conscience connected with evening prayer! When a president of the United States is buried, for five minutes all work stops. All shops close, all trains stop in their track, people stop on the streets. There is silence for five minutes to remind everybody of the great event.

In a similar vein, you also should command total silence for a few minutes every evening. Isolate yourself from the outside world, and conduct a thorough examination of conscience. Of course, you must be rigorously honest with yourself: it is easiest to deceive your own self. What are you going to find in the depth of your soul? Often surprising things. You may have to make a confession like Franklin did after one of his examinations.

"I was astounded to find that I had more errors than I thought; my only satisfaction was that their number was decreasing. I often had the temptation to stop this detailed examination of conscience; it appeared that the rigor and details I demanded of myself was petty pedantry in moral matters. Still, I continued the practice. And although I never reached any perfection for which I was striving–I definitely and greatly fell short of it–still my efforts made me a better and happier man than I would have been otherwise." You may notice, observing yourself, that you suddenly fly into a rage, or you are inclined to laziness, or to lying, or to being sensitive, or to weakness for delicate foods, or to ridiculing others, *etc.* If so, do not quickly reassure yourself like so many other people do: "Nothing can be done! This is my nature! I cannot change my nature!" Not so! That is exactly where self-education should begin. True, you cannot suppress your nature, you cannot forcibly cripple it; but on the other hand you can indeed lift it up, ennoble it–that is to say, educate it. You can practice virtues contrary to these failings and thereby put some order into your disordered inclinations.

Keep a rational order in educating your soul: first of all fight against your faults which you usually commit with full consent of your free will, with full comprehension of your intellect, and over and against the loud objection of your conscience. If you have succeeded against those, next tackle the smaller faults of carelessness and hastiness. And if you have succeeded against those too, finally come the minor imperfections.

If you cannot control yourself, you have no character yet. But it is also true that a precondition of self-control is self-knowledge.

How much pressure can the boiler take? How much fuel is needed for it? Which valve needs to be used most often? Is there visible wear and tear in the machine? Where is oiling most needed? Only the driver of the steam engine, who knows his machine thoroughly, can answer these questions.

So I strongly recommend that you go beyond answering the question: "What sins did I commit today," because, thanks to God, many young men live for months without serious sins; but rather try to answer questions of the following kind: "How could I be so cowardly as to deny my noble principles out of fear of some ridicule? How could I be so tactless as to make insulting statements about my friend to please others? What good could I have done today which I failed to do? How could I have been kinder, more attentive, exact, restrained and forbearing? Have I worked to spread the kingdom of God?" Some of these are not sins, only imperfections capable of eventually distorting your soul. Have no fear of descending into the depth of your soul, even if you find there armies of disgusting centipedes. The more you shine on them the reflector of self-examination, the sooner they die.

The correct way of daily self-examination is not merely taking an inventory of our deeds of the day past, but rather finding the causes of the faults we discovered. I do not only diagnose the problem, but try to answer the question: "What was the reason for my denying my most sacred principles?" The root cause must be located and destroyed.

And while doing that you may make interesting discoveries. "Today I lost my temper several times." Why? Once, because at lunch I had to eat something I did not like; then I was interrupted in my afternoon play that I should go to study; then I could not find my German word-list I prepared even though I turned the whole room upside down for it.

So what are you going to repent? And to avoid in the future? That you were angry? No! Instead that you are spoiled and comfort-loving. That is the root problem that must be removed.

"I got angry today several times." Why? My friend told on me that I got a bad mark in school from algebra; then on the street a kid started making fun of me. What are you going to repent? That you were angry? Instead that you are lazy and selfish. And so on, and so forth with all your faults. Always go after the cause, the root of the problem.

The problem with some young men is that the development of character cannot be achieved quickly. He might be willing to say after taking a deep breath: "From now on I will be a young man of character!" But he is not willing to commit to the slow, uninterrupted, simple work of developing a character. Unfortunately, the great determination counts for little; what matter are the everyday little victories on the way.

You can make your examination of conscience even more successful if, having found the root causes of your faults, you identify the dominant one, and fight against it for several months. The chief goal is to discover which is your dominant fault.

Do you remember what Goliath said to the Israelites? "Choose out a man of you, and let him come down and fight hand to hand. If he be able to fight with me, and kill me, we will be servants to you: but if I prevail against him, and kill him, you shall be servants, and shall serve us" (1 Kings 17:8-9). Goliath is just like your dominant fault. If only you could conquer it! The other faults will readily submit.

Every young man has a dominant fault from which all his frailties originate. One has a quick temper, the other is easily given over to lies ("exaggerates," "tells a fib," "tells a tall tale"), the third is extremely lazy, the fourth is inclined to sensuality, *etc.*

The way to improvement is a declaration of war against your dominant fault! Without compromise! Every morning stop for a moment during your prayer, and–let us assume you have to fight anger–reflect carefully (it only takes a few seconds) how you could get into situations today that would make you lose your temper (at school, during school break, at home with your brothers and sisters). Then you strongly resolve: "No matter what it takes, today I shall resist being angry or truculent. My God, please help me in this!" During the day you renew your resolution several times if necessary. During the evening prayer you examine yourself: did you succeed? If not, tomorrow you will be stronger. If you succeeded, you thank the Lord Jesus for the victory.

In certain monasteries, it is customary to conduct a joint examination of conscience. On a certain day the monks gather together, and each will tell what faults he noticed in others. You also can make use of this very effective method if you have a good friend whose sharp eye is able to detect flaws in you that you are not able to see. Be glad if you have such a friend.

At the Feet of the Lord

This book is coming to an end, and you may be surprised that having presented my thoughts on the formation of character I left to the very end mentioning the most important means, which is the following the ultimate ideal of every human character, Our Lord Jesus

Christ. But it would be a mistake to believe that it was really left to the end. The necessity of the love of God and the recommendation of a deeply religious life underpins the whole book. But I did not write about this more extensively because this book is to be followed by two others: *The Religious Young Man* and *Christ and the Young Man*, which are to be devoted exclusively to this topic.

It can be gathered from every line of this book that to adopt and use the correct principles for life, *i.e.*, to have character, is easiest when the foundation for it is religious. You have read in this book over and over that you have to choose for yourself a well-defined direction, principle, goal and world view for your life, and then you have to follow them without compromise. Neither my readings, my friends nor my trials will make me deviate from them! My life will be happy only if according to Saint Paul (Eph. 3:1) I will become *vinctus Christi*, a prisoner of Christ, *i.e.*, I bind my will to Christ. A truly strong character must be founded on Christ, and the whole life must be built on Him.

The words of Ernst Moritz Arndt (1769-1860) say the same:

> Before men an eagle, before God a worm,
> So you stand in the storm of life.
> Only the one who feels small before God
> Can be powerful among men.
> (Ernst Moritz Arndt)

The strongest wing of human will is prayer, and the best facilitator of all character formation is true religious life, because nowhere do we find such sure setting of goals and motivation for self-education than in the first lines of the catechism: "God made us to know Him, to love Him and to serve Him and thereby to gain the happiness of heaven."

You make progress on your way to building character to the degree that you succeed in conforming your soul to the ultimate ideal, Our Lord Jesus Christ.

Gaudeamus Igitur...

Gaudeamus igitur iuvenes dum sumus, let us rejoice while we are young, says the old student song. And what it says is true. Pure joy strengthens the will. It is the source of energy, it banishes sin. What you do eagerly goes easily:

> Joy and pleasure in a thing
> Makes all troubles insignificant.

Joy is like sunshine; it is the source of vitality. Also, sunshine drives away mold, rotting and foul air; and similarly noble joy banishes the lowly passions leading to sin. But be careful, my son, about what exactly you consider to be joy. It is quite surprising how greatly differing ideas people have on this matter. There are people for whom joy means inebriation, being stupefied by alcohol, a smoke-filled bar, constant revelry, laziness, loitering, unruly screaming, *etc.*

When in fact joy should mean the beauty of a forest filled with birds singing, the fragrance and colors of wild flowers in a summer

bloom, work well done followed by abandonment to well-deserved play. True joy can only come from a clear conscience. If your conscience is accusing you of something, you can only pretend joy.

If you want to find joy in sinful things, read the inscription on a grave of a student in a cemetery in Bologna:

> *O quam fragilis, nosce teipsum, ruit voluptas;*
> Learn how fleeting and perishable all pleasures are.

We can only bemoan a youth impressed by all-night revelry, sleeping through the day, and squandering time and money on such things. Even the pagan Seneca complains:

> Some have reversed the functions of light and darkness;
> they open eyes sodden with yesterday's debauch only
> at the approach of night...
> (*Epist. mor.* 205)

The same can be said about many young men of today. And the Hungarian poet Dániel Berzsenyi (1776-1836) cries that the great deeds of Hungarian history were not done by such weak and enervated youth:

> Different Hungarians fought
> Along Attila when in bloody battles
> his wrath, ready to crash nations,
> opposed half the world.
>
> A different nation shed its blood
> With Arpad, founder of our country,
> Different Hungarians beat Muslim power back
> Under the great Hunyady.
> (Dániel Berzsenyi)

An enormous amount of true and pure joy, noble enthusiasm, much valuable time and a lot of money earned by others are wasted by the pathetic young men who spend their years of studying in all-night revelries. How many promising young men poured their talents into dissolute drinking during their university years. Already Saint Jerome pointed out that drinking inevitably leads to moral fall when he wrote:

> Wine and youth doubly whip up the desire for pleasure.
> (*Epist. ad Eust.*)

Salvianus wrote on the tombstone of the once migthy Roman empire:

> *Sola nos morum nostrorum vitia vicerunt.*
> (*De gubernatione mundi*, 1. 7. c. 23)

> The sole reason of our fall was our lack of morality.

Do not misunderstand me! I do not want you to be vinegar-faced, sullen. I do not say be sad and morose; but when you laugh you should be able to laugh with your whole heart.

I like cheerful, frisky boys, and always worry when I see sad, idle and prematurely old youths. A boy who sits in the corner with a sad face has either his body or his soul sick. So be always a cheerful, smiling young man, always ready to sing.

You may even pretend to be cheerful out of consideration for others even when your heart is bleeding, but this requires unusual willpower. It is very impressive if you can command yourself to be joyous and calm when you would prefer to be sad. To be sad? That should not be tolerated. I should have enough will power to adjust the barometer of my soul to determine what kind of weather should reign over my soul. To be sad? Never.

Never? And what about having committed a sin? Is sadness justified then? Feeling remorse and sorrow for the sin committed is a required part of the sacrament of Penance. But even this is not pure sadness, not impotent lamentation, since it could not then be the source of new life. The tears of sorrow are softened by the rainbow of a new and better life.

My Youth, Come Back for a Word...

Interestingly, nothing more does a grown-up remember more fondly than his youth. He is overcome by emotion when his youth is discussed. Why is that? Youth is the most beautiful phase of human life. Spring is the most attractive season, the season of development and flowering; youth is the spring of life. Just look at the young tree bursting with the energies of growth and youthful health. Ever new areas of the world are opening up before the soul of the young man, his imagination is active, his memory vivid, he rejoices over his present, and tirelessly weaves colorful pictures of the expected future. Much like the tree in its spring flowering.

Another reason youth is beautiful is because it is not yet burdened by the thousand cares of life. "But I do have cares," cries one of them, "the algebra problem to solve, the language essay to write." May these be your biggest problems ever. But it is well this way. Youth should not be burdened by any heavier cares.

And by a youth without cares I do not mean youth without thoughts. Some people think "freedom from cares" is a synonym for "carelessness." These are the ones who do not use their youth well, and carelessly squander those years that will never return. Yet if you do not use your youth according to the plan of God, *i.e.*, as a preparation for a fruitful manhood, then your youth is a confused dream followed by a bitter awakening.

Keep in mind that *ut flos vel ventus, sic transit nostra iuventus*–youth passes away like a flower or a thunderstorm.

I know very well: a just man shall fall seven times (Proverbs 24:16), and young men tend to fall in the moral life. It is a sad fate, but a human fate, and it does not yet mean moral corruption. I only despair over a soul that refuses to fight the passions and rather backs down in a cowardly manner; who knows how imperfect he is but does not care about it; who does not take self-education seriously.

My ideal is the "young man of character." He can focus his will power, he can control his senses, he can conquer his cowardliness and softness. He values his immortal soul, and can fight for its purity. He cultivates his intellect, and after intensive studying he can still smile radiantly. My ideal is the youth who is most diligent when he studies, who is most fervent when he prays, and who is most cheerful when he plays. What would you like to be?

What Do You Want to Be?

What do you want to be? You might think I enquire about your career selection. But no. I am not asking if you want to be a medical doctor, a merchant, an engineer, a priest, a lawyer or a tradesman. Wherever your wishes, calling, circumstances take you, it is all equally good for society. But what is important is that once you decide on your chosen post, you should be a whole man there, fulfilling all your duties.

So when I ask in parting what you want to be, I am really asking if you have thought about what is man's end or mission in this world. Because everything in this world, even the smallest insect or speck of dust, has a purpose, a significance, and a connection with the whole created universe. In certain cases, it is hard to comprehend this purpose and connection, but it exists nevertheless.

And only man would not have a purpose? Oh, yes, and what a magnificent one! So what is your purpose? The glory of God and your own happiness. What does that mean? It means that you have to strive to fully realize your essential being and the meaning of your life. In other words, you have to become a young man of character. A Catholic young man of character.

Who is a man of character? Someone who has the strength to resist every kind of moral corruption. And who is a Catholic man of character? Someone who in this deceitful world, where everybody tries to appear to be something else than what he really is, is trying to shape his soul with unswerving determination into a character staunchly devoted to truth. You should work with all the steadfast determination of your young soul to become exactly such a Catholic.

In Ancient Rome a grand temple was built to all the gods, and was called the Pantheon. The gods of all the religions of all the conquered people were gathered together, and the temple was filled with innumerable idols, one stranger than the other. This magnificent building filled with idols represented the confusion and uncertain gropings of the human spirit.

One day, at the beginning of the fourth century, travelers from a distant land arrived in Rome; they were Christians. They entered the Pantheon, and when looking around at all the grinning idols there, a great unnameable sadness engulfed them. One of them took out a small crucifix, and having put the humble little crucifix down among the giant idols, they all left in silence.

This story represents the struggle of the Catholic young man of today in the pantheon of modern idols. When you finish school and enter life, your soul will also encounter the cold wind of modern paganism. You will realize that the world full of scrambling, pushing, and trampling is really a pagan pantheon full of idols with hideous grins; and unfortunately people are doing homage to them, and the only one getting less and less homage is the true God. And willy-nilly you will have to join this paganism. You will have to enter this pantheon, except that you are not allowed to become a pagan.

If you, my dear son, will carry on your breast and in your soul the cross of Our Lord Jesus Christ, and you will live in that spirit in today's world, by doing so you place the crucifix in the middle of the modern pagan world, into your immediate society, among your fellows, your acquaintances, your friends, your workplace and the neighborhood you live in. This is the way you will radiate light, joy and a good example; this is how you will become a "man of character" from a "young man of character."

A Sad New Year's Eve

Do not forget, my son, the thought that speaks to you from every sentence of this book: You have a treasure in you more valuable than anything conceivable, which is your immortal soul. The task of your earthly life is to make your soul the most ideal, the most beautiful, the most rich with noble qualities. Your eternal life will correspond to the perfection of your soul that you managed to accomplish in this earthly life.

There is an interesting plant called the agave. A version of it, *agave americana*, is also called the "Century Plant" because this plant takes a long time to flower. The name seems to imply that it flowers once in a hundred years, although the number of years before flowering occurs depends on the vigor of the individual, the richness of the soil and the climate; during these years the plant is storing in its fleshy leaves the nourishment required for the effort of flowering.

So the agave can be thought of as flowering once in a hundred years, but then its flower is very beautiful. It is preparing for this unique day, it is collecting its forces to make itself beautiful for a hundred years. And when the time arrives, this plant enchants its viewers.

My dear son! You should become like this agave. Devote all your energies to accomplishing the great goal: I have to become a character! I am a growing tree! I am a ripening crop! In my youth I have to work incessantly on my soul eventually to become a man of character that will please even the angels in heaven.

The soul must be conquered, and the price of the conquest is struggle. The desires of the body go against the noble strivings of the soul, and struggle breaks out. The great freedom fight of the soul! What is at stake is who is to rule: my soul or my body? What is at stake is who is to command: the master or the servant? What is at stake is who is at the helm of the ship: the captain or the deckhand? What is at stake is which way the ship of my life is to go: to be lost among rocks and cliffs always in danger of running aground or heading straight for the home port? And finally, what is at stake is where this ship is to land: on the shores of eternal happiness or in the hopelessness of eternal perdition?

Well, this is a goal well worth fighting for!

The famous German writer Jean Paul (1763-1825), born Johann Paul Friedrich Richter, describes the hopeless state of a soul who suffered a shipwreck of his faith. On New Year's Eve an old lonely man is contemplating from the window of his room the motionless, bright, starry sky and the silent earth covered with white snow. There is not another man in the whole world with as desolate a heart as his. His grave is about to open up before him, he is getting closer to it by the day, and he notes with terror that from his long life he brought nothing with him but a mass of missteps, sins, and illnesses, a body crippled by pleasures and a soul poisoned.

In his memory the days of his youth are swirling like frightening ghosts, the wonderful May morning when he first set out on the road of an unknown life, and the fateful moment in which he, the youth of much promise, left the rocky road of duty, morals, honor and work and chose instead the treacherous road of sin promising pleasures but in reality leading to destruction. Pain is tearing the heart of the white-haired man as he cries in the silent night: "Oh, if only my youth would come back just once more! My Father, give me another chance to choose differently!"

The complaints of the crying old man are swallowed up without an answer by the freezing silence of the winter night. He has no more chance to choose...

But for you, my son, having to make the choice is still before you. You can still make the right choice.

> Do not be spring–without flowers!
> Do not be sky–without stars!
> Do not be a young man–without noble ideals!

> Can I choose?
> Well, here it is: I choose!
> I want to be a young man of character!

I intend to live so that all my thoughts, words and deeds will be a credit to me on the Great Day of Accounting; so that I may be counted worthy to hear the happy invitation from Our Lord Jesus Christ:

> Come, ye blessed of my Father, possess you the kingdom
> prepared for you from the foundation of the world.
> (Matt. 25:34).

Yes, I will stand on the side of the Lord, and will never be disloyal and untrue to Him.

Never, ever!